JAF CLI   JAFFREY M
CLIMBING THE MANGO TREES

CLIMBING THE MANGO TREES

Madhur Jaffrey

CLIMBING THE MANGO TREES

A Memoir of a Childhood in India

EBURY
PRESS

First published in Great Britain in 2005

1 3 5 7 9 10 8 6 4 2

First published by Ebury Publishing
Random House UK Ltd, Random House,
Vauxhall Bridge Road, London SW1V 2SA

Random House Australia (Pty) Limited
20 Alfred Street, Milsons Point, Sydney,
New South Wales 2061, Australia

Random House New Zealand Limited
18 Poland Road, Glenfield, Auckland 10, New Zealand

Random House South Africa (Pty) Limited
Isle of Houghton Corner Boundary Road & Carse O'Gowrie,
Houghton, 2198, South Africa

Random House UK Limited Reg. No. 954009
www.randomhouse.co.uk

A CIP catalogue record for this book is available from the British Library

EDITOR: Michelle Turney
DESIGNER: Peter Ward

ISBN: 0 0918 9929 X

The photograph on the endpapers shows the family posing for a picture at a picnic on New Year's Day, 1928, at the 12th-century monument of Qutb Minar, Old Delhi

Papers used by Ebury are natural, recyclable products made from wood grown in sustainable forests.

Printed and bound in Great Britain by Clays of St Ives.

This book is dedicated to

Bari Bauwa and Babaji,

My Grandparents,

For

Helping make their grandchildren who we all are

And

To my daughters

Sakina, Meera, and Zia

And their cousins,

As well as

To my grandchildren

Jamila, Cassius, and Rohan

For

Carrying on the line of the inkpot and quill set

So bravely

And so innocently

CONTENTS

My Family Tree   viii

Prologue   xi

Chapters 1 – 29   1 – 218

Epilogue   225

Family Recipes   233

Author's
Acknowledgements   267

Publisher's
Acknowledgements   269

About the Author   271

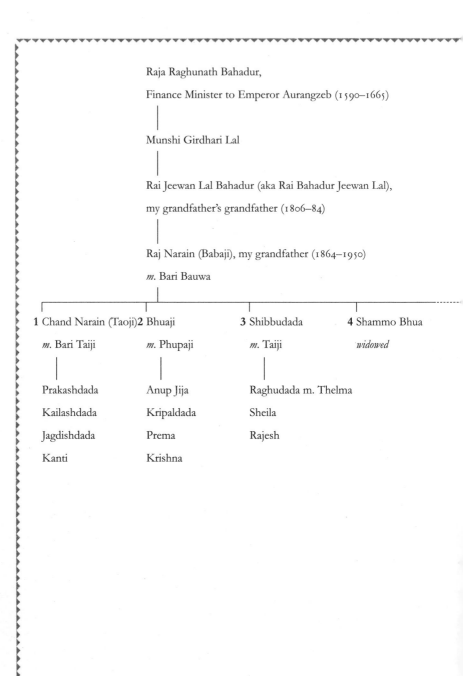

Raja Raghunath Bahadur,
Finance Minister to Emperor Aurangzeb (1590–1665)

Munshi Girdhari Lal

Rai Jeewan Lal Bahadur (aka Rai Bahadur Jeewan Lal),
my grandfather's grandfather (1806–84)

Raj Narain (Babaji), my grandfather (1864–1950)
m. Bari Bauwa

1 Chand Narain (Taoji)	**2** Bhuaji	**3** Shibbudada	**4** Shammo Bhua
m. Bari Taiji	*m.* Phupaji	*m.* Taiji	*widowed*
Prakashdada	Anup Jija	Raghudada m. Thelma	
Kailashdada	Kripaldada	Sheila	
Jagdishdada	Prema	Rajesh	
Kanti	Krishna		

MY FAMILY TREE

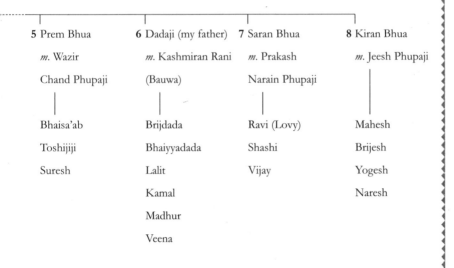

5 Prem Bhua	**6** Dadaji (my father)	**7** Saran Bhua	**8** Kiran Bhua
m. Wazir Chand Phupaji	*m.* Kashmiran Rani (Bauwa)	*m.* Prakash Narain Phupaji	*m.* Jeesh Phupaji
Bhaisa'ab	Brijdada	Ravi (Lovy)	Mahesh
Toshijiji	Bhaiyyadada	Shashi	Brijesh
Suresh	Lalit	Vijay	Yogesh
	Kamal		Naresh
	Madhur		
	Veena		

PROLOGUE

Goddess or Sweet as Honey? ❈ *Winter: The Season of Weddings*
The Caterer as Magician ❈ *Lessons in Taste*

I was born in my grandparents' sprawling house by the Yamuna River in Delhi. Grandmother welcomed me into this world by writing 'Om', which means 'I am' in Sanskrit, on my tongue with a little finger dipped in honey.

Perhaps that moment was reinforced in my tiny head a month or so later when the family priest came to draw up my horoscope. He scribbled astrological symbols on a long scroll, and declared that my name should be 'Indrani' or 'Goddess of the Heavens'. My father, who never paid religious functionaries the slightest bit of attention, firmly named me 'Madhur', which means 'sweet as honey', an adjective from the Sanskrit noun 'madhu' or 'honey'. Apparently my grandfather teased my father, saying that he should have named me 'Manbhari' or 'I am sated' instead, as I was already the fifth child. But my father continued to procreate and I was left with honey on my palate and in my deepest soul.

My sweet tooth stayed firmly in control until the age of four when, emulating the passions of grown-ups, I began to explore the hot and the sour. My grandfather had built his house in what was once a thriving orchard of jujubes, mulberries, tamarinds and mangoes. His numerous grandchildren, like flocks of hungry birds, attacked the mangoes while they were still green and sour. As grown-ups snored through the hot afternoons in rooms cooled with wetted, sweet-smelling, vetiver curtains, the unsupervised children were on every branch of every mango tree armed with a ground mixture of salt, pepper, red chillies and roasted cumin. The older children on the higher branches peeled and sliced the mangoes with penknives and passed the slices down to the smaller fry on the lower branches. We dipped the slices into our spice mixture and ate; as our mouths tingled, we felt initiated into the world of grown-ups.

Winters were another matter. That was when the vegetable garden came into its own. Around eleven each morning, between breakfast and lunch, we would be served fresh tomato juice. At about the same time, the gardener would offer the ladies sunning themselves on the verandah a basket full of fresh peas, small kohlrabis, white radishes and feathery chickpea shoots. Some of these we ate raw and the rest were sent off to the kitchen after a studied appraisal ('Radishes sweeter than last year, no?'). As this was also the season when the men went hunting, the kitchen was deluged with mallards, geese, quail, partridge and venison as well.

Dinners were fairly generous affairs with about forty or more members of the extended family sitting down to venison kebabs laden with cardamom, tiny quail with hints of cinnamon, chickpea shoots stir-fried with green chillies and ginger, and small new potatoes browned with flecks of cumin and mango powder.

Winter was also the season of weddings. My father was in charge of the caterers and I was his permanent sidekick. In those days caterers had to cook at home and, certainly in our home, they had to cook under family supervision. So a gang of about a dozen caterers would arrive a few days before the wedding and set up their tent under the tamarind tree.

First, my father would examine all the raw ingredients. Were the spices 'wormy'? Were there broken grains in the basmati rice? Were the cauliflower heads taut and young?

The outward suspicion from one side and obsequious reassurances from the other were a game each side dutifully played. In reality, we loved these caterers, who were known for the magic in their hands. They could conjure up the lamb meatballs of our erstwhile Moghul emperors and the tamarind chutneys of the street with equal ease. One of the few dishes that they alone cooked was cauliflower stems. For one meal they would cook the cauliflower heads. Then they were left with hundreds of coarse central stems. They cleverly slit them into quarters and stir-fried them in giant wok-like *karhais* with sprinklings of cumin, coriander, chillies, ginger and lots of sour mango powder. All we had to do was place a stem in our mouths, clamp down with our teeth and pull. Just as with artichoke leaves, all the spicy flesh would remain on our tongues as the coarse skin was drawn away and discarded.

Decades later, in New York City, I helped culinary guru James Beard – my friend and neighbour – teach some of his last classes when he was very ill. One of them was on taste. The students were made to taste nine different types of caviar and a variety of olive oils, and do a blind identification of meats with all their fat removed. Towards the end of the class, this big, frail man confined to a high director's chair asked, 'Do you think there is such a thing as taste memory?'

This set me thinking. Once, several of us who had known each other for decades were sitting by a fireplace in France, talking and reading. My American husband, a violinist, was studying the score of Bach's *Chaconne*. 'Can you hear the music as you read it?' a friend asked.

It was the same question in another form. When I left India to study in England, I could not cook at all but my palette had already recorded millions of flavours. From cumin to ginger, they were all in my head, waiting to be called to service. Rather like my husband, I could even 'hear' the honey on my tongue.

CHAPTER ONE

---

*Delhi – Old and New * Sir Edwin Lutyens and the
House that Never Was * Babaji * Number 7
The Lady in White * The Kite*

The orchard site had housed our family homestead only since the early decades of the twentieth century. My family came from the walled city, often called Old Delhi, just to the south, built by the Moghul emperor Shah Jahan in the seventeenth century. My family referred to it simply as 'Shahar' or 'the city'.

There are many Delhis, as we were to study in school, built either alongside or wholly or partly on top of each other, often reusing materials from buildings knocked down in bloody efforts at domination. Our original family home was in Chailpuri, in the narrow lanes of the Old City. As its carefully chosen foundation, it had sturdy stones 'borrowed' from the walls of Ferozshah Kotla, the fourteenth-century fortress and emperor's palace.

Starting with the ancient Vedic city of Indraprastha that flourished in the fifteenth century BC, a succession of Delhis was built first by generations of Hindu rajas, only to be followed in AD 1193 by a roll call of Muslim dynasties: Ghori, Ghaznavi, Qutubshahi, Khilji, Tughlak, Lodhi and Moghul. They seemed to trust the dubious comfort of walled cities, and their leaders chose to name Delhi, again and again, after themselves. This ended, at least from my childhood point of view, with the British version, sans walls –

New Delhi – designed by Sir Edwin Lutyens and built in the ruin-filled wilderness south of the Old City walls.

The Moghul capital Shahjahanabad, or Shahar, was where the written history of my family began. We were blessed only with our paternal side of it. My mother's side either kept few records or humbly kept its accomplishments under wraps. This written history, bound in red, was kept in my grandfather's home office.

When my grandfather – Babaji as we called him – decided to move out of the city to the orchard estate, he was already a very successful barrister. His new house, the one in which I was born, was a brick and plaster version of a multi-roomed, grand Moghul tent with bits of British fortress and Graeco-Roman classicism thrown in to hint vaguely at grandeur. The road it was built on was named after my grandfather, Raj Narain Road (with the patriotic Hindification of names that followed Independence, it is now Raj Narain Marg), and had the number seven on its front gate. From the time I can remember, we always referred to that house as Number 7, as in 'I'm going to Number 7' or 'You know that big tamarind tree in Number 7 . . .'

Not wishing to waste money, and full of the brio of one recently 'England-returned' (he had been studying law in London), my grandfather designed it all himself. As the family story goes, it was at this time that the British had decided to move their capital from Calcutta to Delhi, and Lutyens was in the process of building the new capital, to be named New Delhi. Lutyens asked my grandfather to pick any piece of land there and build on it – Lutyens might have designed the house himself had my grandfather asked – but my grandfather dismissed the whole idea, saying, 'Who wants to live in that jungle!' Properties in 'that jungle' are now worth as much as those in central London and Manhattan.

Number 7, Delhi, so nearly designed by Lutyens. In front of the house stands our beri *(jujube) tree in which we loved to sit as children. All the young of my generation had our favourite, reserved spots among the branches.*

Years later, having proceeded beyond my three score and ten years, I was awarded an honorary CBE (Commander of the Order of the British Empire) by Queen Elizabeth II in Washington, DC, another city designed by Lutyens. The ceremony took place in a house also designed by Lutyens, the British Ambassador's residence. As I stared at my reflection there in a pair of dark Lutyens mirrors dotted with glass rosettes, I couldn't help thinking that my life might have come full circle. I could have been born in a Lutyens house and received a grand recognition of my life in a Lutyens house. But I was not destined for such easy symmetry, for easy anything.

Babaji's whitewashed house consisted of a central gallery, a hall really, leading to five very large rooms with fireplaces. One of these was the drawing room, and the others served as bedrooms, one to a family. Running along the front and back of the house were two long verandahs lined with semi-classical pillars. The back, east-facing verandah looked out on the Yamuna River, or, as we called it with great familiarity, the Jumna. It was here that so many of us, as infants, were rubbed with oil and left to absorb the morning sun. Because the land must have sloped down to the water, this verandah was one floor up, built over a large, partially underground cellar or *taikhana*. Before I was born, my grandfather used to make wine from grapes he imported from Afghanistan in this permanently damp, cool place.

The front, west-facing verandah looked over the gardens, which had incorporated the remnants of the old orchard and now included a winding drive to the front gate. The front and back verandahs ended with rooms at each corner of the house, the front ones shaped somewhat like turrets. The functions of these corner rooms changed over the years but one of them at the back, facing east and south, always remained my grandmother's – and the family's – chapel-like *Pooja ka Kamra* or prayer room. On the top of the house were two levels of flat roofs, the one in the centre being higher, both edged with a battlement-like balustrade.

But the main house was not large enough to fit the only army Babaji was to see, a growing army of spirited grandchildren produced by his eight children. Some of these progeny lived at Number 7 all the time, while others came and went. Babaji firmly believed in the joint family system, with himself presiding as the head of his brood, a system that had been followed by his father and grandfather and, indeed, by all his ancestors.

So, in addition to the main house and gardens, across two vast brick courtyards to the north and south of the main house were two long, train-like annexes. One-room wide and made of brick, they had a more casual, country feel. The one to the north started at the river end with the dining room and then went on to pantries, storage rooms and the kitchen. Beyond it, across another bit of courtyard on the same north side, was the boiler, industrial in size and used for making extra hot water for our winter baths, and an annexe of bath-rooms. The annexe to the south, known simply as 'the rooms' (*Kamras*), also started at the river end. It contained my middle uncle's bedroom and offices, my grandfather's offices and then extra rooms for guests. Besides all this there was a shed for cows and horses plus a servants' annexe and two sets of large garages.

It was in my grandfather's southern annexe office that I one day discovered, by complete chance, a book bound in red that was the family's history. (I must have been thirteen at the time.)

There were actually two types of family history. There was the documented version that sat properly in my grandfather's office. But there was also the undocumented version consisting of fables, family customs and hearsay passed along by my grandmother, Bari Bauwa, and the other women of the house. This version had begun seeping into us since birth, very subtly, with the honey on our tongues. And, to start with, this was the only one I knew.

Every year, at the religious festival of Dussehra in autumn, Bari Bauwa would demand that we bring all our writing implements to the prayer room. The men would be asked to bring their guns as well. She would arrange these in the altar-like temple she had set up: Parker pens, bottles of blue-black Quink, pencils, hunting rifles, all mixed in with gods, sacred threads and marigolds. The women and children would gather inside the prayer room, with the men always hovering, unconvinced, by the doors. We would begin praying and sprinkling these rather ordinary implements with yellow turmeric powder, red *roli* powder, grains of rice, holy water and flower petals. I thought then that all of India was doing what we were doing: asking blessings for pens and pencils and guns.

What I did not realize was that on that day, most Hindus were asking God to bless the implements they worked with. Farmers wanted blessings for their bulls and ploughs, and traders for their weights, measures and coins.

But who were we and why was my bottle of Quink in the prayer room? According to the women's oral history – and this was never taught to us, just deduced slowly over time – we were a sub-caste of Hindus known as Kayasthas, Mathur Kayasthas to get the sub-, sub-caste right. Even as a child, I saw it so clearly in my imagination . . . Roll the film: Ancient India. Day. A vast meeting of notables is being held on a mountainside to finalize the caste system. At the top of the heap, it is announced, are to be the self-satisfied priests, the Brahmins, who will be the only ones allowed the privilege of reading, writing and making laws. There is much cheering from their quarter. Below them are to be the warriors, Kshatriyas, who will fight and rule kingdoms. This lot seems overjoyed too. Lower on the totem pole will be the traders and farmers, Vaishyas, whose eyes glint at the thought of making money; and even further down, the menial workers or Shudras, who stand glum and silent.

The camera shifts. Next day. Night. A small hall lit with oil lamps. A smaller meeting of agitated intellectuals. They are overwrought because they are viscerally against all these categories. In any case, they do not fit neatly into any of them. Reading, writing and making laws are what gives them the most satisfaction but religious orthodoxy scares them and they want none of it. They have no fear at all of ruling any part of the world but they will not give up their precious books. They lack both the sort of entrepreneurial spirit that makes successful traders (in fact, hush, they look down on traders), and the physical strength and desperation that sustains farmers. So they vote rather boldly to form a union of their own, a separate sub-caste of free-thinking writer-warriors to be known as Kayasthas. The End.

That is my version of events. There is actually a real legend, if legends can be real, that goes something like this. Just after Brahma, the God of the Universe, had created the caste system with, in descending order, the Brahmins, Kshatriyas, Vaishyas and Shudras, a worried Yama, God and Chief Justice of the Underworld, approached him saying, 'I need an assistant who has the ability to record the deeds of man, both good and evil, and to administer justice.' Brahma went into a trance. When he opened his eyes he saw before him a glorious figure of a man holding a pen in one hand, an ink-pot in another and a sword tied around his waist. Brahma spoke, 'Thou hast been created from my body (*kaya*), therefore thy progeny shall be known as Kayasthas. Thy work will be to dispense justice and punish those that violate Divine laws.' Brahma gave him the special caste of Dwij-Kshatriya, twice-born warrior.

Another such 'history' lesson came directly from my grandmother. I will never forget the day.

It was one of those sunny but crisp, cold winter Sundays that Delhi loves. Winter lasted only two months and our family turned quite British for this season, at least in our clothing. All the tweed coats and jackets (British fabrics, Indian tailors) and cardigans (British wool and patterns, family women knitters) came out of mothballed trunks. They were spread out on the lawn and sunned repeatedly for days in a desperate effort to rid them of their naphthalene odour, after which they were hung or folded up and put into cupboards. The women wore hand-knitted cardigans on top of their sarees and then bundled themselves further in Kashmiri shawls.

I was ten and looking smart as smart can be in my pale-blue herringbone-patterned woollen overcoat, made to measure at Lokenath's in Connaught Place, New Delhi (my two older sisters had exactly the same coats). It was January and so cold that we had to wear overcoats both inside and outside the house. I smelled of mothballs.

About twenty of us had barely collected in the dining room annexe for breakfast when the Lady in White arrived. Of the same age as my grandmother, she was habitually enshrouded in a long white skirt or *lahanga*, a white bodice and a white covering over her head. Her skin colour matched her clothing. I used to think that my mother was the whitest Indian I knew until I met the Lady in White. My mother was the colour of cream. The Lady in White was the colour of milk. What mattered most to us, though, was not her milky colour but the milky ambrosia she carried on her head.

Yes, balanced there, on a round brass tray, were dozens of *mutkainas*, terracotta cups, filled with *daulat-ki-chaat*, which could be translated as 'a snack of wealth'. Some cynic, who assumed that all wealth was ephemeral, must have named it. It was, indeed, the most ephemeral of fairy dishes, a frothy evanescence that disappeared as soon it touched the tongue, a winter speciality requiring dew as an ingredient. Whenever I asked the Lady in White how it was made she would sigh a mysterious sigh and say, 'Oh child, I am one of the few women left in the whole city of Delhi who can make this. I am so old and it is such hard work. What shall I tell you? I only go through all this trouble because I have served your grandmother from the time she lived in the Old City. First I take rich milk and add dried sea foam to it. Then I pour the mixture into nicely washed terracotta cups that I get directly from the potter. I have to climb up the stairs to the roof and leave the cups in the chill night air. Now, the most important element is the dew. If there is no dew, the froth will not form. If there is too much dew, that is also bad. The dew you have to leave to the gods. In the early morning, if the froth is good, I sprinkle the cups with a little sugar, a little *khurchan* [milk boiled down into thin, sweet, flaky sheets] and fine shavings of pistachios. That, I suppose, is it.'

Those cups were the first things placed before us at breakfast that day. Our spoons, provided by the Lady in White, were the traditional flat pieces of bamboo. Heavenly froth, tasting a bit of the bamboo, a bit of the terracotta, a bit sweet and a bit nutty – surely this was the food of angels.

But it finished too fast. After every bit had been licked up, we were still hungry so orders went out to the kitchen. *Karara* (crisp on the edges) fried eggs; rumble tumble (scrambled) eggs with tomato, onions and green chilli; rumble tumble with tomato, no onion, green chilli and green coriander; masala (spiced) omelette with bacon.

All the eggs were served with toast. That day, my cousin Rajesh, the youngest son of my middle uncle, downed his breakfast and dashed outside. I, his devout follower, still had most of my toast left to finish. I just grabbed it in one hand and ran after him.

We both raced through the northern brick courtyard, heading towards the gardens. Just above the northwestern turret room was a tall electric pole where a kite had made its perch. That moment, the kite saw fit to swoop down and take my toast away from me, leaving, thank God, my eye whole but a deep, bleeding gash just under it. Then it swooped back up to its perch. I screamed and my cousin, startled out of his wits and feeling deeply responsible, rushed inside for his 22 Daisy air rifle, which he aimed and fired. His pellets missed but the noise and commotion brought the whole family out into the courtyard. He was lectured by his mother, I by my mother and both of us by our grandmother. What my grandmother, Bari Bauwa, had to say was much more than a simple admonition. My cousin, she said, had almost killed the saviour and patron of our *kul*, our clan.

Then she told us this story. In ancient times, when much of north India was divided into small principalities, our ancestors were the rulers of a kingdom called Kukraj, somewhere near Jaipur in Rajasthan. There was a devastating war with a neighbouring raja and our entire clan was massacred, all save an infant boy whose mother had fled with him to a nearby town called Narnaul. The only reason he survived was because a big kite flew down, landed on the ground and spread her wings over him, shielding him from view – and harm. The family priests immediately decided that if the boy lived, they would declare the kite *kuldevmata* or tutelary goddess of his family. The boy lived and his descendants took to treating all kites with the deepest reverence.

It was in the early summer three years later that I discovered the red leather-bound book, the real history of our family, in my grandfather's office.

CHAPTER TWO

Summer Lunch ❊ *The Red Book*
The Story of my Ancestors ❊ *Muslim Influence*

We were still in Delhi and had not yet left for our annual
holidays in the hills. My grandfather's short, gnarled
manservant, Ishri, always in his old-fashioned *dhoti*
and with most teeth missing, had announced lunch. As usual, the
family crossed the northern courtyard in small groups and trooped
into the dining room annexe. This day we lunched on fresh *phulkas*
(fluffed, whole-wheat flatbreads); *alan ka saag*, (a kind of dal made
with chickpea flour, *moong dal* and spinach), eaten with squeezes of
fresh lime juice; small bitter gourds stuffed with fennel and browned
onions; home-made yoghurt and *kakris*, long, pencil-thin, curling-
at-the-end summer cucumbers, eaten raw with their delicate, pale
green skins still on. These were hawked in the streets of Delhi with
the enticement, '*Laila ki unglian hain, Majnu ki pasliyan*' ('These are
the fingers of Juliet, the ribs of Romeo'). We ended the summer
meal with bunches of fresh lychees from Dehradun and tiny, sweet
melons posted to us from Lucknow by my father's second-youngest
sister, Saran Bhua. We were all so full. The elders had ambled off to
their bedrooms, their heads already leaning towards their pillows.

Most summer afternoons, the children were free of all adult
supervision. This day, even my cousins must have fallen prey to
lethargy as I distinctly remember being alone.

As a child, I was very happy being alone. We were surrounded by so much love, concern, family tensions, cousinly competition, and the general goings-on of a large joint family, that it was almost a relief to paint all that out. I would instinctively change gear and, within seconds, reach a silent zone I kept for myself where I was welcomed by a blank canvas. I was free to fill this with new, shifting dreams.

It was in such a state of half-wakefulness that I walked across the front of the house, unlatched the door to my grandfather's office and entered.

I often went there when I was alone. Babaji himself hardly ever used the place any more. Ishri, his manservant, had given up his regular dustings so a thin layer of sand from the Rajasthani desert had crept under the door and spread its gritty self on the big desk in the centre of the room, the brass duplicating machine on top of the desk and all the bookshelves.

The dust did not bother me. I made the duplicating machine go up and down a few times, I opened and shut the desk drawers and rummaged through my grandfather's papers. Then I went to my accustomed spot near the farthest bookshelf and sat down on the floor.

Most of the cases held legal tomes. But in one of the lower shelves, filling its entire length, was a series of large volumes called *The Books of Knowledge*. I had already read them all from cover to cover many times over. I had read about Marconi and Marie Curie, about Laplanders and Pharaohs and every Greek myth the books could supply. I was planning on reading about Adonis again when my eye fell on a red cover nearby. I reached for and pulled out that book.

I loved history in school. India was still a colony so we were taught British history, of course, but Indian history as well. What I was holding in my hand was a history all of my own with familiar family names, a book in which the two histories I was studying in school seemed to merge.

The cover indicated that the book was a 'Short Account of the Life and Works of Rai Jeewan Lal Bahadur , Late Honorary Magistrate, Delhi, with Extracts from his Diary Relating to the Time of Mutiny, 1857'.

Rai Bahadur Jeewan Lal, also known as Rai Jeewan Lal Bahadur, was my grandfather's grandfather, born on 2 April 1806. Luckily for us, the book contained relevant details of recorded family history that preceded Jeewan Lal, and went beyond his death to the time when my own grandfather turned twenty-one. It covered almost a century.

I read it over several afternoons, respectfully returning it to its place each time. After my grandfather's death in 1950, an aunt sold the entire contents of the office to the *kabaaria* or rubbish man. Books by the yard. Pages from our history may have been used as plates to sell snacks in the city. Spicy, potato and pea-filled samosas oozing their grease on 'By command of his Excellency the Viceroy and Governor-general, this certificate is presented in the name of her Most Gracious Majesty Victoria, Empress of India, To Rai Jeewan Lal . . .' Or perhaps some family member had quietly walked off with it before it could suffer such an ignominious fate. At any rate it disappeared from my life. Another fifty years would elapse before I would see it again: not the original, but a reprint.

The book – clear, precise and filled with copies of letters and documents to substantiate all claims – was put together by one of Jeewan Lal's sons. It began, strangely enough, in mythology, retelling my grandmother's story about the kingdom of Kukraj, the infant boy and the kite in a slightly different version. But then it tried to imbue the myth with a modicum of weight by adding that in Jeewan Lal's time, an ancient piece of wood, tied with an equally ancient piece of thread, known always as the throne (*Kukraj ki Patri*) as well as the family protectress – the kite – were included in all domestic prayers.

Whatever the truth of these old beliefs, the family's real story began in the seventeenth century. Our ancestor, Raja Raghunath Bahadur, left his home town, Narnaul, north of Jaipur, and came to the glittering Delhi court of the Moghul Emperor of India, Shah Jahan. The city – Shahjahanabad then – was completely walled. The emperor, a direct descendant of Genghis Khan and Tamerlane, lived and worked in the Red Fort and ruled from his famed peacock throne. The throne boasted six solid gold feet and encrustations of rubies, emeralds and diamonds, including the Koh-i-Noor diamond, now broken up and in Queen Elizabeth II's crown.

Raghunath Bahadur would not have been allowed just to walk into the court of the 'grand Moghul', one of the world's richest and most powerful emperors. This was a time when the emperor could be approached only with eyes lowered to the ground and full cognizance of the Persian couplet, 'Should the king say that it is night at noon/Be sure to cry, Behold the moon'. There were already other, lesser members of our Kayastha community toiling in the court: 'The Hindus [read Kayasthas] took so zealously to Persian education, that, before another century had elapsed, they had fully come up to the Muhammadans (Muslims) in point of literary acquirements', doing much of the revenue collection, account keeping and official court correspondence.

My ancestor's way into the Moghul court was eased by the sponsorship and patronage of the finance minister, Asadullah Khan, who soon appointed him his deputy. As Shah Jahan aged and the bloody wars of succession between his sons began, Raghunath Bahadur was shrewd enough to align himself with the eventual victor, Aurangzeb. When emperor, Aurangzeb amply rewarded him for his sagacity with titles, money, an army of 2500 horsemen and, on Asadullah Khan's death, the post of finance minister.

Aurangzeb was the last of the grand Moghuls. Europeans – the English, French and Dutch – had begun encroaching as early as the fifteenth century, desirous of enriching themselves in the spice trade. By now, they were on a roll; they had set up well-fortified colonies in major port cities and moved inland, warring with local chieftains and with each other. The Moghul Empire was falling apart. All the major movers and shakers in the Moghul court were leaving to set up their own kingdoms. One branch of my family took off with the general who would form the southern princely state of Hyderabad, and ran the revenue department. My own ancestors went on to work in another Muslim court nearby, that of the Nawab of Kunjpura (in Haryana today).

Hindu India was under the domination of Muslim rulers from the late twelfth century until the nineteenth century. What struck me as I sat reading on the floor of Babaji's office was that my family, without being told, never ceased fulfilling its destiny as scribes. Were we choosing freely? Or was Brahma, with the image of the man with the quill and ink-pot firmly before him, tugging at strings attached to the right side of our brains, generation after generation?

At a time when most Hindu families kept their distance from Muslim families, ours not only went to work for Muslim rulers but also mastered their court language, Persian, with such zeal that we were relied upon to write history, keep records and manage taxes and accounts.

This Muslim influence did not just stay at the office. It went to the core of the men's being, affecting their etiquette and manners, even their courtship. When they came home, they changed into Muslim-style clothes – white-on-white *kurtas* embroidered in Lucknow on top of loose white pyjamas – and amused themselves with recitations of Persian poetry, some of which they wrote themselves, and the pursuit of art and literature. Indeed, when my grandfather's grandfather Rai Bahadur Jeewan Lal died, the *Statesman*, dated 3 May 1884, declared his collection of old and rare Persian books, architectural plans and miniature paintings to be most valuable and unique and that 'in him we have lost perhaps the best informed student of Indian history in North India'.

I remember once, just before the Partition of India in 1947, when Hindu–Muslim angers were running deep, a Hindu school friend chastised me for being too 'broad-minded', as if it were a sin. She then dismissed me saying, 'Well you Mathur Kayasthas are half-Muslim anyway!'

There was indeed a strong overlay of Muslim culture in our house and a genuine spirit of tolerance towards all faiths, leading to a strange split between the highly educated men and the less educated women. If the men spoke Persian and Urdu, the women kept up their Hindi and read the holy *Ramayana* from front to back each year. If the men drank and ate kebabs, the women served them willingly enough but went back into the kitchen to prepare meals that included *kadhi* (a thick chickpea flour soup with dumplings), potatoes with ginger and summer squashes with tomato and cumin.

The women's clothing was a mixture of Muslim and Hindu. My mother and all my aunts were raised wearing the *izaars* and *kurtis* of

My eldest aunt, Bhuaji, 13 years old, on her wedding day.
She wears fashionable izaars *(culottes) in rich damask and is laden with jewellery,*
including a gold jhumar *(head ornament) in Muslim style, a large gold*
nose ring and six pairs of anklets.

the Muslim world, culotte-like loose trousers either embroidered for special occasions or made of chintz with small thigh-length shirts. Once they married, they moved on to *lahangas*, traditional Hindu long skirts. They did not wear the more modern saree until the 1920s when my grandfather bought identical sarees by the dozen and doled them out to all the women of the house.

In spite of the Islamic overlay, neither the men nor the women ever veered from being completely Hindu. Jeewan Lal may have been a great Persian scholar but he was also a master of Sanskrit. If the men greeted their friends raising a hand to the forehead in a very Muslim salaam or *aadaab*, they greeted the family with joint palms and a solid, '*Jai Ramji Ki*' ('Praise be to Lord Rama').

Yet another influence was to enter our family's life: that of the British. Were we going to turn half-British too?

CHAPTER THREE

*British Rule ❋ The Record-keeper ❋ Mutiny of 1857
The Reward*

When British rule was extended to Delhi in the latter part of the nineteenth century, the court of a Resident (best compared to a governor) was established there. The British capital remained, for the time being, in Calcutta. Many of the Indian rulers, struggling for influence with the newest power, sent emissaries to the court of the Resident of Delhi. The Nawab of Kunjpura sent a trusted lawyer, Girdhari Lal, the father of the main character in our family history book, Jeewan Lal. The Resident, Sir D. Ochterlony, took to him to such an extent that he tried to poach him with the offer of a job as his *Munshi* or record-keeper. Feeling he would be disloyal to the Nawab at a critical time in the nation's history, Girdhari Lal refused but cleverly suggested his son for the job, saying that the Resident would get two for the price of one as he would naturally give his son all necessary assistance. And so Jeewan Lal came to be employed by the British, first under Sir Ochterlony and then Sir T.T. Metcalfe, rising to the rank of *Mir Munshi*, chief record-keeper and honorary magistrate. The men of our family who once knew Persian now had also learnt English. The British side of our family saga had begun.

We now reach the period of the 1857 Mutiny. The British declared it a mutiny as it started with a rebellion by Indian foot-soldiers, Hindus and Muslims alike, angry at being forced to use cow and pig grease on their bullets. It soon grew into a protracted and very bloody nationwide insurrection against the British, a long series of battles joined on the Indian side by provincial chiefs, nawabs, rajas, masses of Indian soldiers and common folk. The Moghul Emperor dithered at first but joined the rebellion in the end. Many decades later, the first Indian Prime Minister, Jawaharlal Nehru, was to call this the first Indian War of Independence.

The colonial rulers prevailed, though not without the help of 'loyalists' like Jeewan Lal. For this and his general services, Jeewan Lal was given the title of 'Rai Bahadur' by the Viceroy and Governor-General of India, Lord Lytton. (The Moghul Emperor was banished to Burma. Nearly all the citizens of Delhi were expelled.) Jeewan Lal was also offered a substantial reward but he turned it down, saying that he had more than enough for his needs.

This refusal was to haunt the family later as it fell on hard times. As a loyalist, Rai Bahadur Jeewan Lal had suffered irreparable losses during the Mutiny. Here I quote from his diary:

11 MAY 1857: . . . Sohan [a servant] also stated that he heard the city *badmashes* [miscreants], who were pointing out to the rebels the abode of the nobles of the town, utter my name also, and say that they should repair to the house of the *Mir Munshi* of the Agent and Commissioner and plunder it. 'I tell you for the sake of loyalty,' said Sohan, 'that you close the gates of your house and put heavy locks on them so that no *badmash* may enter the house and create disturbance.' Accordingly, the writer forthwith made the necessary arrangements. Although the house I lived in was very spacious and strong like a fort and had very large stones from the Kotla [Fortress] of Ferozshah put in its foundation . . . I found it advisable to lock both the gates and put heavy locks on them. I hid myself in the dark *taikhana* [cellar] built of the same

stones and above it stationed my servants as guards to keep watch and give me information if any persons came here . . . and considering for what a long time I have been eating the salt of the Government, and was its well-wisher, and that this was a time to repay it all and try with my heart and soul for my masters, I appointed the same Sohan to go to Sir John Metcalfe . . . tender my respects to them and ask them to give me orders for whatever service they might wish me to perform.

12 MAY: Two Mooglee Telungas [rebel soldiers] came to my house and made disturbance. [We] paid them four rupees and made them go away.

13 MAY: Two other rebel soldiers entered my house, and took away my goods, viz, carpet, door, pillows, books and one box containing cash and jewels and shawls etc., value 2000 rupees.

19 MAY: [Miscreants] reached my house by climbing from roof to roof of adjacent houses, and plundered it, taking away women's jewels, carpets etc., value 2500 rupees.

23 MAY: Rebel soldiers, hearing that I was sending news to the British officers, and being exasperated at their fruitless search after me, demolished all the buildings in my garden, and plucked off fruit from trees, inflicting a loss of 3000 rupees.

1 JULY: Bahadur, gardener, came and reported that the rebels had gone to my garden . . . cut down the trees and carried them away.

19 JULY: . . . came to me wearing the king's [Moghul Emperor's] livery and threatened me saying, 'the king's rule is now established, not a trace of the English is left, your *kamra* [city room/office] in Chandni Chowk [the main street in the Old City] is in my possession, bring out the title deeds etc. and deliver them to me . . . So I gave him the title deeds and wrote the lease upon which he became the owner of my premises worth 5000 rupees.

1 AUGUST: The king's officials . . . demand that I present myself with 50,000 rupees. I recite the following verse in my mind: 'God rescue me from this trouble/No one (but thee) knows what is passing in my mind.'

4 AUGUST: Nazir Ali, Thanedar [jail superintendent] of the emperor, came to arrest me . . . accompanied by 100 rebel soldiers with unsheathed swords in their hands . . . The females of my family were sitting by Maharaja Lal [his second son] who was suffering dreadfully in those days, the stone having been recently extracted from his bladder, and ran pell-mell to the upper storey at the sight of the rebels. The rebels took away the *paandan* [the box used for betel leaves] containing jewels left by the females. The writer was arrested, and being placed in a palanquin, was carried under the escort of the rebels, holding naked swords in hand, to the *kotwali* [police station]. [Here] an old *subedar* [sergeant] . . . ran up to stab me with his drawn dagger, shouting, 'This is the man that sends news to the English.' [Jeewan Lal was rescued by a Moghul friend.]

It was the custom then for one man – the head of a household that included all children and grandchildren – to be responsible for all of them, financially and otherwise. The family coffers had been emptied during the Mutiny. Rai Bahadur Jeewan Lal's death in 1884 was followed, soon after, by that of his eldest son. His next son, Maharaja Lal, unable to work because of severe deafness, appealed to the British Government for the reward the family had once refused. He asked that the younger generation, which included my grandfather, be given a chance to sit the entrance examinations at London law schools.

My grandfather, Raj Narain, was barely twenty-one and already a student at St Stephen's College in Delhi. His college also submitted a petition to the British Government for him. In the end my grandfather did go to London, and the reward, consisting of land and villages outside Delhi, did come through. Some of this was sold and the money used both for education and to purchase the orchard

*My grandparents, circa 1926, some of the clan and the two Number 7 family dogs.
The sarees were ordered in bulk by my grandfather and are here worn in the
old-fashioned way. Back row: Prakashdada, Saran Bhua, Shibbudada, Taoji,
my father, Kiran Bhua. Middle row: Bhuaji, Taiji (Shibbudada's wife), Bari Taiji
(Chand Narain's wife), Babaji, Bari Bauwa, my mother, Shammo Bhua.
Front row: Anup Jija, Raghudada, Kripaldada, Prem Bhua,
Harish Bhaisa'ab, Kailashdada, Brijdada.*

estate, a huge piece of land procured by the joint family and then
divided up between them. My grandfather ended up with a choice,
curving plot overlooking the Yamuna River, Number 7. His younger
brother lived next door in Number 16, his elder brother's family
was down the road in Number 8 and his cousins in Number 4 and
so on. The numbers were picked haphazardly, according to personal
preferences. Our entire neighbourhood consisted of family, several
generations in each large house.

CHAPTER FOUR

The Freedom of Kanpur ❋ *My Mother and Father*
A Fairy-tale Marriage ❋ *A Desire to Excel*

My birth took place in my grandfather's orchard house on 13 August 1933, the night of Janmashtmi, the dark eighth day of the waning moon, the feast day of Lord Krishna's birth. I was delivered by Dr Keany, a British missionary lady-doctor, as my sister, Kamal, was banging at the door and crying because she was not allowed in. In the India of that time you were what your family was (I borrow shamelessly from Brilliat Savarin) and my family was a hybrid: it was Hindu by origin but heavily veneered with Muslim culture and English education; it considered itself very liberal but lived by the ancient rules of the joint family system where men dominated, where only men made it to history books, and where all marriages were with other Kayasthas – more ink-pot and quill. I may have been born with honey on my tongue but I was also born squirming against the status quo.

When I was about two years of age, my father took a job as the manager of a *ghee* (clarified butter) factory. This was not real *ghee* but the hydrogenated cooking oil variety, a kind of shortening known in India as *Vanaspati*. The factory, Ganesh flour Mills, was owned by my father's cousins; in fact, the cousins who lived at Number 4, so it was all in the family. However, the factory was not in Delhi but in Kanpur (Cawnpore in those days), an overnight journey by train.

My father, mother, me, Kamal and Lalit
on holiday in the hills in about 1936.

All through my grown-up life I have written many times about
Kanpur but I have rarely identified it. I have always merged it with
Delhi. They were really quite distinct. But in my childhood
memory, we would leave the house in Kanpur, get into our car, drive
along the gardens, through the high, gated walls and go to sleep in a
train; then pass through a less severe, white-painted gate, down
another drive and there, in front of us, was the Delhi house, Number
7. Both houses were our homes and they were seamlessly adjacent.

My parents, whom we called Dadaji and Bauwa, had five
children at this stage: my two older brothers Brij and Bhaiyya, my

*Left to right: Lalit, Kamal and me (eating an apple)
in the garden at Kanpur. I am about five.*

sisters Lalit and Kamal and me. Brijdada and Bhaiyyadada (the
'dada' was added out of respect for our elders) were twelve and ten
years old respectively and already going through the rigours of
Delhi's Modern School. Pulling them out was considered a very bad
idea so they were left under the general supervision of the joint
family with my middle uncle, Shibbudada, keeping a special eye on
them. At just two, my schooling had not even begun. Lalit at seven
and Kamal at five were at Queen Mary's School but so bright that a
move for them at that age was not considered a problem at all.

Kanpur was such a happy time for my parents. My father was
freed from playing second fiddle to his autocratic father and his
highly popular, music-loving, entrepreneurial middle brother,
Shibbudada. My mother did not have to be a dutiful daughter-in-law,

sister-in-law or aunt. She could just be a mother and wife. Kanpur was the only place my parents thrived.

Even though they were in Kanpur for eight years, Delhi remained their official home. My grandfather would not have it otherwise and loosened the strings only so far. Every holiday we returned to Delhi, to the room in which I was born that balanced out my grandfather's large room at the back of the house. When my father wanted to buy a separate house in New Delhi for himself, my grandfather said no and my father fell silent. That is how the joint family system, the respect-for-elders routine, worked.

My father, Dadaji, was one of the best-looking men I knew. He was tall – well, tall-ish by Western standards – about five feet eleven, straight-backed and even-featured with fine dark hair that he parted on the side and then brushed backwards with his English brushes. His clothes were British, all arranged very neatly on hangers by my mother: tweeds for the winter and khakis for the summer. For formal occasions he had Muslim-style *achkans* (like Nehru jackets but knee-length) in different weights of wool and cotton, which he wore with tight *churidar pajamas* (tight poplin leggings with extra folds at the bottom). He dressed, smoked and drove his ever-changing British and American cars with the style of a man about town.

My mother was just as short as my father was tall, barely five feet, so she always wore heels to compensate. When she was born, she was so startlingly light-skinned that her family bestowed upon her the name Kashmiran Rani (Queen of Kashmir), which signified the height of beauty. Her face, as sweet and open as her nature, could be classified as softly pretty, but in the India of that time the colour and smoothness of her skin were enough to lift her into a special class of the 'highly desirable'.

She too dressed with uncommon flair. Although her taste was

My parents, stylish in their summer whites,
in the mango orchard of Number 7.

impeccable, she lacked my father's flamboyance, perhaps because
of her size and rounded frame. She wore only sarees: cottons in
the day; printed silks for simple shopping excursions, chiffons,
georgettes and heavy Benarasi or south Indian silks for evening
parties. Her cupboards were as neat as my father's – naturally, as she
was everybody's cupboard-keeper. The cottons, nicely starched by
the *dhobi* (washerman), were stacked one on top of the other on
shelves; the everyday silks were on hangers; but a very special
treatment was reserved for the dressier sarees.

My meticulous mother would first get rectangles of heavy cardboard, all cut to the same size, about sixteen by thirteen inches.
She covered each with sturdy brown paper. She would then take a
saree and fold it into a very long rectangle the same width as the card-

board, place the cardboard in the centre of this rectangle and fold the saree over it in thirds. That was not all. Muslin, bought by the bolt, had been cut into large squares. Each folded saree was now enfolded again in the muslin, like putting a letter in a freshly made envelope.

Bauwa had hundreds of heavy, dressy sarees. Some that she wore regularly were in her cupboard, and others not in use were stashed away in trunks. When she needed to wear one, it came out of the muslin, off the cardboard and was then draped on her body as she stood in front of her long dressing table mirror. When she returned home, she undraped the saree, folded it up, put it on the cardboard and wrapped it back in muslin. The girls, generally in identical dresses, stood in a row and watched. We, her daughters, have most of her sarees now. They are all in perfect condition.

Sometimes in Kanpur, when my mother was sitting on a *takht* (divan), her legs folded to one side, doing her repairing on a small Singer sewing machine, I would ask her for the umpteenth time to tell me how she came to marry my father. She was still filled with the wonder of it all. For me, the story was more moving than anything in Grimm's *Fairy Tales*. It was an arranged marriage of course.

In the Old City of Delhi, there were two large families living just a few narrow lanes apart. One was rich and powerful. The other was humble but good. Their paths rarely crossed as the rich family was always busy with important government officials, university people and industrialists.

One day, when the handsome youngest son of the rich family had just finished college, his father approached him saying, 'Son, it is time for you to marry. As is the tradition amongst us, we have asked the barber to nose around and find a girl who is worthy of you.' 'I am perfectly willing to marry,' the handsome son said, 'but I want a girl who is beautiful, sweet-natured, bright and talented. Is this at all possible?' 'We can only try,' replied his father.

The barber-matchmaker was dispatched. He went to Agra and did not find anyone. He went to Jaipur and did not find anyone. He went to Lucknow and Allahabad and saw no-one who fitted the handsome son's desires. The barber returned to the Old City and reported to the father, 'I am sorry to bring bad news but such a girl does not exist.'

Just then, the handsome boy's sister spoke up. 'But I know such a girl. She is my friend. She went to school with me. The barber should look there. It is just a few minutes' walk from here.'

The barber talked to the girl's parents and asked for her horoscope. Then he returned to the rich family's home and handed the horoscope to the handsome boy's parents. 'Now, I have done my work. If the girl's horoscope matches with that of your son, we are in business.'

The horoscopes matched perfectly. A wedding was arranged. But the girl had never even set eyes on the boy.

One day the handsome son's sister went to play with her friend at the humble family's home. They were eating some squiggly jalebis (pretzel-like sweets filled with syrup) when the sister looked out of the window and saw her handsome brother walking by. 'Look, look, look,' she said to her humble friend, 'There, outside the window, is the man you are about to marry.' The humble girl looked out and was astounded. 'Why, he is a prince,' she exclaimed.

On the wedding day, as the sound of the *shehnai* (oboe-like instrument) that led the wedding procession got closer and closer, the humble girl's heart beat faster and faster. Her prince was approaching on a big white horse and he would take her away . . .

That was my mother's version of the story as told to a little girl. But the truth was that she never stopped thinking of my father as the prince who had, by some miracle, taken her to his heart. She stepped lightly through life, feeling no urge to leave an imprint. My prince-like father, on the other hand, was totally dependent on her quiet strength. In our large joint family with many strange marriages, my parents' union seemed the most comfortable and joyous.

They were, in many respects, quite different from each other. My father had a BA degree from St Stephen's College and spoke English fluently. He liked to read biographies and histories and to study maps. He smoked, and listened to the BBC news in the evenings as he drank his whisky and soda. He played bridge and tennis at the club and loved to hunt and fish with his friends. He enjoyed good food, especially the meats, *pullaos* and breads that came with our Islamic veneer.

My mother was 'eighth-class-pass', which meant she had not even gone to secondary school. She spoke no English. Whenever the rest of the family went on for too long in English, she would say in Hindi, '*Arey Ram* (Oh God), so much git-pit, git-pit, git-pit.' That was what English sounded like to her. But, rather like an English mother whose children can natter away in French, she also looked pleased. Pleased to have lucked-out with this git-pitting group.

My mother's uncommon intelligence made up for her lack of schooling. After she died we found in her neat cupboard, still laid out with pride, several silver medals she had won in school for top scholastic honours. In those days, it was not thought necessary for girls to study for too long. After all, their only purpose was to be married off. Whatever my mother did do, however, she did to perfection. She cooked the foods my father loved plus all the traditional Hindu festival foods: *papris* (chickpea flour poppadums) for Holi, the spring festival; glazed lotus seeds for Janmashtmi, the birthday of Lord Krishna; and *puas* (sweet whole-wheat dumplings) for Karvachauth, the day women prayed for their husbands. She sewed, she knitted, she embroidered with silk and gold thread, not just ordinary things but extraordinary creations. I have had one of them framed: a set of finely wrought gold-thread and sequin crowns she made for herself and her first-born to wear at a horoscope naming ceremony.

I feel I inherited my mother's desire to excel. But where she quietly accepted the limitations of her times, I was given the luxury of rebellion by very loving and indulgent parents. The fifth child and a girl, I was way beyond the heir and the spare. They could take a chance with me as they could not with their older ones.

CHAPTER FIVE

Choosing a School ❀ A Milky Nation: the Milk Beauty
Secret and Milk for Breakfast ❀ Our Morning Rituals
The Magic Garden

My memory begins in earnest at about the age of four. We were in Kanpur. Dadaji, determined that his daughters should be as well-educated as his sons, had explored Kanpur schools and had come up with two very different options. There was the Mahila Vidyalay, an all-girls school where every subject was taught in Hindi and the emphasis was on Hinduism and Indian traditions. Then there was St Mary's Convent, a coeducational school, at least until the middle grades, where most of the teachers were German and Irish nuns, the medium of instruction was English and the education was basically Western and, of course, Christian.

I remember my father driving us slowly past the Mahila Vidyalay again and again, as if just by looking at the school and the girls who came rushing out he would be able to divine its suitability for his daughters. I think that a part of him, the part that was fighting for Indian independence as a member of the Indian Congress Party, would have liked us to go there. But the girls at the Vidyalay seemed to lack the all-round sophistication he thought we should have, and in the end he put my two older sisters in the Convent. He trusted us to withstand the tsunamis of Westernization and Christianity, and to hold on to our Indian-ness as he and his father before him had managed to do. His approach contained inherent contradictions, but that was how we seemed to live our lives.

Bauwa woke us early each morning, only to rush us to the sink in our bathroom to brush our teeth and do our 'milk cleansing'. When it came to make-up, my mother had a simple, minimal style. There was her *bindi*, the dot of red powder (*sindhoor*) she put between her brows; the kohl she made herself by burning camphor under an upturned terracotta bowl, collecting the soot and adding oils to it, which she used to line her eyes (and ours); and there was the Hazeline Vanishing Cream, which she put on her face. When she went out, she dabbed a few drops of Evening in Paris perfume on her neck from a small blue bottle.

I have no idea where she picked up the milk 'beauty secret', or why she set so much store by it. Perhaps my father offhandedly mentioned to her that Cleopatra bathed in ass's milk. Perhaps she was made to do it as a little girl and it really was some ancient family beauty secret. She never explained, we never asked and in India you never know. She did have a convincing air of authority about her, and who could question a walking advertisement for perfect skin?

There would be a bowl of fresh cow's milk waiting at the sink. Rich and creamy, it came from our cows that had been milked at dawn, delivered by the *gwala* or cowherd. First we splashed this on to our faces. Big white blobs of it clung to our lashes. Then we had to rub the milk in with our fingers, back and forth until it dried and came off in little dirty threads. We could now wash our faces with warm water and our skin was soft and smooth!

After our baths, my mother went off to pray in the little section of the storeroom she had decorated with her *pooja* (worship) paraphernalia; she watered the *tulsi* (holy basil) plant and then helped her husband and daughters get ready for work and school.

For breakfast, the girls and Bauwa always had tall glasses of milk. My mother never developed a taste for tea or coffee though she served them at all proper occasions in the prettiest English porcelain. We had hot milk in the winter and cold in the summer. Those who wished could add Ovaltine to it, although I never did. The milk came from the same cows that had provided our beauty treatment. India is a milky nation: milk with sugar; milk with saffron and nuts; tea with milk or cream; yoghurt with fruit, nuts, vegetables, dumplings and rice; steamed yoghurt; hung-up yoghurt; fresh milk cheese (*paneer*); fresh milk cheese sweets from *rasgullas* to *chum chums*; milky rice puddings (*kheer* and *phirni*); and milk ices and ice creams. Without milk, India, this highly lactosed country, would just wither away.

My father had tea, two fried eggs and toast for breakfast, day after day. He ate the whites of the eggs first. Round and round he'd go with his fork and knife, the whites slowly disappearing, until all that was left were two glistening yellow orbs, shaking like jelly on his white plate. He would pick up one whole yolk on his fork and slip it into his mouth. He would chew it slowly, the blue vein at his temple throbbing in rhythm. Then he would pick up the second yolk. All activity stopped as we gazed in wonderment.

With our milk we sometimes had bread and cheese, sometimes just fruit and sometimes eggs sprinkled with my mother's special salt that was always kept in small cut-glass containers on the table. The recipe, apparently, was my grandmother's and consisted of salt, pepper and ground roasted cumin seeds. Except on special weekends, breakfast was Western, with jams in proper cut-glass, silver-lidded jars, toast in silver toast-racks, Kraft cheese straight out of a tin – tins were considered modern and exotic – Marmite housed in its traditional dark-brown jar and, every now and then, ham, bacon or sausages bought from Valerio's, a speciality bakery and meat shop owned by a Goan couple, Mr and Mrs Noronha.

One car with a driver then took my sisters to school. My father either drove himself to his office or he walked: the office was right inside the walled compound that included the *ghee* factory and the homes of other, lesser officers of the company.

My day was then all my own and I spent it mostly in the garden. Perhaps I should say 'gardens' as there were several of them, including vast lawns, a badminton court, a tennis court, a rose garden, mixed flower borders edged with sweet peas, and several gardens devoted to just flowers and vegetables. We grew not only almost every kind of flower that might flourish in our subtropical climate, from cannas to lupins, but all our own vegetables too – potatoes, onions, carrots, okra, aubergines, cauliflowers, cabbages, kohlrabi, peas and tomatoes. There was a head *mali* (gardener) with assistants to do the hard labour, but all the designing, choosing of trees, ordering of seeds and planting was managed by my father, whose chief passion in life, other than his family, was his garden.

At one end of the compound was the cowshed, the most distant area of the garden. I visited this several times a day. A long, narrow path led up to it, formed by the high brick wall, hedges and trees on one side and an endless trellis of green beans on the other. I would skip along the path or ride my tricycle along it, breaking off beans and nibbling them as I went. Dadaji had created such a complete universe for us. For a dreamy little girl growing up, it lacked absolutely nothing. There were the specially ordered 'black' roses that were really a deep purple; the snapdragons that could be made to 'bark' by pinching the flowers in the middle; and the marigolds whose centres we called coconuts and devoured. But there were also little corners of the garden where I could escape, lean my head against a tree and vanish in a kaleidoscopic world of English knights and princesses, Indian gods with multiple arms, Bombay movie heroes, Indian detectives from my mother's nightly readings-aloud of Hindi detective stories, and characters from British and American comic books.

At the cowshed the tethered cows would be engrossed in licking hunks of rock salt suspended before them with wire. Like determined sculptors, they would lick and lick with their coarse tongues, smoothing out all rough edges until creations worthy of Henry Moore would magically appear. Every day I would note the changes and marvel at their ravishing forms.

I would then rush to observe the daily churning of butter. It was done just outside the pantry on the bricked, covered pathway leading to the kitchen. We only ate white, homemade butter. I did not know any other kind existed. We would smear the butter thickly on our toast, sometimes with salt and pepper on it. The milk was poured into a round earthenware pot to which the wooden churner was attached. As ropes pulled the churner this way and that, little bits of white butter flew out onto the ground, and crows would gather to eat it. One day, as I watched, I decided to shoo the crows away. Most looked angrily at me and left but one stayed. I took a step forward to shoo it. The crow took two steps forward in defiance. I ran away in fear.

All morning I wandered around with the *mali*, dogging his footsteps. I carried salt and pepper with me so I could season and then bite into a red-ripe tomato still smelling of its green sepals. I helped dig up tiny potatoes and broke off the sweetest green peas, shelling and eating half of them while throwing the rest into the *mali*'s basket. And I helped pick the prickly okra which, when cooked and combined with the equally glutinous split-pea, *urad dal*, sent me into paroxysms of ecstasy. (Perhaps that accounts for my partiality to Japanese glutinous foods like mountain yam and fermented beans, *natto*.) When the *mali* went to the massive pit that held the manure and organic leafy matter, there I was watching him turn the compost around. I could not leave the *mali* alone even when he ate his lunch.

He always settled down to eat near the shady water tank. I followed him there. First he would wash his hands and feet and dry them off. Then he would sit down with a deep sigh, throwing all the weight of the world off his shoulders, and open up a small cloth bundle to reveal two thick whole-wheat *rotis* (flat breads), some raw sliced onion and some green chillies. I would sit down with him, leaning against the same brick wall. Bauwa had warned me not to take the *mali*'s food but the *mali* was too generous and I was too greedy. I never took too much. Just a bite. All I know is that nothing tasted more heavenly than that simple combination. Years later as I travelled the world, I would compare this to the pasta with olive oil, garlic and red chilli I had in Italy or the plain rice with chilli *sambal* I had in an Indonesian village – the wonder of basic, national starches enhanced with only the simplest of local seasonings.

In our Kanpur home, my mother had the daily task of keeping household accounts. In the morning she would give the cook a list of what was needed and the money to buy it. Generally, it was just meat and spices as we produced all dairy goods and vegetables ourselves, and buying fruit was my father's responsibility. The cook would then go off on his bicycle. On his return he would have to recite what he had bought and what it cost as my mother, sitting on her bed with her knees pulled up, wrote it all down in the endless registers she filled up in Hindi. The smallest item, and its price, was noted down. Even salt. She may not have had much education but she did not have ancestral ink flowing through her veins for nothing. Her job, our job, was to keep records.

When my father returned from work, we all gathered around him as he had his tea. The girls were subjected to their second glass of milk of the day. If it was summer, I sat out on the back lawn watching my parents and sisters try their hand at badminton, or my father teaching the girls how to ride a bicycle, while I listened to the crickets. As we built up a sweat, we were allowed cooling fresh lemonades (*neebu ka sharbat*), fruit squashes (fruit syrups diluted with iced water) and that new-fangled drink, Vimto, as well. If it was winter, my father stayed indoors listening to the news on his Phillips radio. War was on the horizon and my father did not like what he was hearing.

CHAPTER SIX

Summer Holiday ❈ Baby Sister
Starting School and Learning English ❈ The Toffee Man
The Quest for Barley Sugar ❈ My Perfect Sisters

My younger sister was born when I was five, just before the first salvos of World War II, during our summer holiday in Dalhousie. This hill station was built on three Himalayan peaks at about 7000 feet above sea level and named after a British governor-general in India, the tenth Earl of Dalhousie.

The large house we had rented that year was named, rather grandly, Teera Hall. As usual, the entire extended family was present, with a few dozen – including my mother – sleeping in a large dormitory-like room on the second floor. As my sister was expected, a hill palanquin (*daandee*) was kept at the ready to take my mother to hospital if needed. But my sister was born suddenly during the night. At first we were all asked to cover our heads with our quilts, and then my mother was rushed to my grandmother's room adjacent to ours. I could hear her moaning gently. Every now and then her door would fly open and an aunt would rush out for hot water or towels, shutting the door behind her. I was frightened out of my wits. Then I heard an infant crying. The door opened. A weary aunt stepped out and whispered to a cousin who ran down the room yelling, 'She's been born, he's been born' ('*Ho gai, ho gya*'). He'd been told of a birth but not the sex of the child.

I started school the year my sister Veena was born and my father began to worry seriously about the war. At the age of five, like my sisters before me, I was thrown into an English-speaking class of Indians, Anglo-Indians and Britons. Until then, I had spoken to my mother and the servants in Hindustani. My father and sisters switched languages when speaking to me or to my mother, so even though I had heard English spoken all around me, I could not speak a word of it myself.

But I learned fast. Rather like learning to swim by being dropped in at the deep end of a pool, within a month I surfaced speaking the language of our colonial masters. I could 'git-pit' with the rest of them.

My school years in Kanpur were, like everything else in our lives, sometimes severely compartmentalized and sometimes a zany mix-and-match of cultures. In the mornings we put on our white blouses, navy blue tunics, socks and tightly laced shoes, which my mother double-knotted. We were *never* going to lose these shoes! We couldn't even get out of them. Our coconut-oiled hair was parted in the middle, braided tightly into two pigtails and secured firmly at the bottom ends with black ribbons. Our pigtails were not going to come loose either.

My mother handed us our khaki solar *topees* (hard, brimmed hats) and our rigid leather school bags filled with textbooks she had covered with brown paper. Then she escorted us to the car, her lightly starched cotton voile saree crackling as she walked.

Once we got out of our front gate, however, we were in charge. We instructed the driver to go 'faster, faster'. The aim was to be at top speed as we reached a small, arched bridge over a narrow tributary of

My sisters Lalit (to my left) and Kamal and me (aged about four), wearing my favourite red dress, in the back garden of the house in Kanpur.

the Ganges. At that speed, the car went up the bridge and then flew. Our stomachs lurched and we held our breath until we landed with a bit of a thud. Not very good for the car but it made our morning and prepared us for the nuns!

Our convent school, quite naturally, recognized only one religion: Catholicism. If you weren't a Catholic, you couldn't go to the chapel for Mass in the morning. This was a bit of a disappointment as the chapel always looked and smelled so, well, holy. Instead, all non-Catholics – the few Hindus and Parsis and many Anglo-Indian Protestants – had to attend Bible history class held in our everyday classrooms. I enjoyed reading the King James Bible. Even more, I enjoyed the free exchange of holy pictures afterwards. I liked to collect the slightly raised ones printed on hard, smooth cardboard, outlined with gilt.

At school we recited 'Half a pound of tuppenny rice, half a pound of treacle' and 'Four and twenty blackbirds baked in a pie' as if to the manor born, even though we had never eaten a pie in our lives and had no real sense of what treacle was. At morning break, we were allowed to use the small daily allowance given by our mother, about two annas each (an anna was a sixteenth of a rupee), on goods offered by the Toffee Man. This was the highlight of the school day.

The Toffee Man was Indian but had been vetted by the nuns. He sat cross-legged on the stone floor of a back verandah, his home-made wares taken out of a tin trunk, spread on a cloth in front of him and sold to us on squares of paper. And what wares: half-pink, half-white coconut toffees, cut in diamond shapes that melted in the mouth; chocolate toffees cut in thin squares that were part fudge and part caramel; and the barley sugar . . . fat twists and rough, dimpled balls of candy in yellow, orange and red, opaque on the outside, translucent inside, not too brittle but hard to bite off, and once in the mouth, teeth-sticking and chewy. These were treats only the Toffee Man had. They disappeared from our lives after St Mary's Convent.

Not entirely. Years later, in the 1980s, I was in Calcutta's covered New Market researching a cookery book and preparing to film Merchant Ivory's *Heat and Dust* in Hyderabad a week later, after a stop in Delhi. I looked at the fish shops selling Bengal's famed *rahu* (a kind of carp) and *hilsa* (a shad-like mackerel), and the men who shopped for them in the early hours of the morning. I went to the spice shops to examine Bengal's five-spice mixture that once included the now disappearing spice, *radhuni*. All of a sudden, something made me turn my head and there, across a narrow market lane, was a shop that announced 'Barley Sugar'. It just could not be true. Barley sugar labels had deceived my sisters and I many times before. It always turned out to be some brittle, machine-made rubbish that lacked the chewy texture and very slightly caramelized taste of the real thing. Barley sugar was now a mirage, surely.

I crossed the narrow lane anyway. Lord, it looked like the real thing. Fat, twisted sticks, misshapen dimpled balls. I tasted a piece. This was it! The Anglo-Indian owners had been making and selling it for decades. I could have kissed them. I bought several pounds of it, carrying it on the plane to Delhi to offer to my sister Kamal. She was sceptical at first, having been deceived many times before, but one bite convinced her. Kanpur came rolling back and the two of us went out of our minds. Even though we admonished each other with, 'Are you crazy? It's pure sugar,' we behaved like children and managed to finish every last bit of the barley sugar in less than a week. I personally put on six pounds, which I had to get rid of with a month-long diet of just tandoori chicken and salad at my Hyderabad hotel.

At school, the Toffee Man was followed by arithmetic, which I loathed, English – reading, essay-writing or dictation – which I loved, and nature study, which was a great favourite as it allowed me to both draw and write. By then it was lunchtime. My sisters and I would meet up again as our food was freshly made and came in a four-tiered tiffin-carrier from home. Our turbaned bearer brought it in the car.

One of the school's side verandahs was lined with benches and tables for all the children whose food came from home. The bearers spread out tablecloths and set the crockery, cutlery and napkins before the end of the last class. As my sisters and I came flying out, our bearer would open up the tiffin-carrier and spread out the containers, putting a serving spoon in each of them. The food was still warm. There might be *koftas* with cinnamon and cardamom in one, rice with peas or chapatis in another, cauliflower with potatoes in a third and perhaps homemade yoghurt or a salad in a fourth. Afterwards there was some easy-to-eat-fruit such as bananas or Indian oranges, which are like large, loose-skinned tangerines.

I was very curious to see what those around me were being served. Some children had sandwiches. Tomato and cheese was popular, as was the spiced egg sandwich. Some children had leftover roasts from the night before. One Anglo-Indian girl with thin brown hair who sat at the bench next to me always startled me with unusual combinations. I remember looking over once and seeing the following on her plate: at nine o'clock there were cornflakes; at twelve o'clock there was plain rice; at three o'clock there was cooked *masoor dal* flowing slightly into the rice; and at six o'clock there was an English sausage. She ate all this with a fork and spoon.

After lunch there was drill (*up, two, three, four; down, two, three, four; feet astride, two, three, four*), singing (hated it) or needlework (loved it but

*I joined the Bluebirds (a sort of junior Guides) while a pupil
at St Mary's Convent in Kanpur. I am in the front row, fourth from the left;
Kamal is in the back row, second from the left.*

hated needle-nosed Sister Alberta who taught it: 'WHAT did you say? WHAT DID YOU SAY? Get up young lady. You will NOT say "thanks". The word is "thank-you". Say "thank-you, Sister". Stand up and put your needlework down. Now. Put your needlework down NOW.'), history or geography (loved both) and library, where I took out as many books as possible, the whole world of English classics.

After school, the car would bring us back home. I would tear off my uniform, my shoes and socks, fling down my hat and bag, put on *chappals* (backless sandals) and a cotton frock of my mother's design and, with my sisters, make a dash through the dining room into the pantry. Whoever got there first got the end of the bread loaf.

I don't know who started this but I suspect it was my sister Lalit. My mother now had our baby sister, Veena, to look after so she often rested in the afternoon. All the servants were off taking a break as well. Knowing how hungry we would be when we came home from school, my mother would leave food in the cast-iron warming oven, whatever she and my father had eaten for lunch, generally a meat – my father rarely ate a meal without meat – some goat and potato curry and some chapatis. At first we used to roll the meat up in a chapati and eat it in a form my mother called a *batta*. Then my sisters began improving on the chapati roll. They ignored the chapati completely. Instead, they cut the thickest end slice from a loaf of bread and hollowed it out, removing most but not all of the soft portion. Into this crusty 'container' they first put a layer of meat, then potatoes, then mango or lime or chilli pickle. As my sisters could run much faster than me, they generally ended up with both crusty ends of the loaf while I was left with the softer middle, but often they were known to share.

That was the trouble with my two older sisters. They were models of decorum and decency: thoughtful, fair, polite, pretty, demure, softly-spoken and considerate. If I was hurt and angry, I bawled and beat my fists; they cried softly into their pillows. If I rode first our tricycle and then our 'lady's' bike like a fiend, they wafted along on them like dainty clouds. If I complained about the behaviour of an uncle or cousin, they pointed out the good side. If I was the somewhat unruly Elizabeth Bennet, they were versions of Jane Bennet. If I was Jo in Little Women, they were just as clearly an amalgam of Margaret and Beth. I was doomed by comparison (yet you see how I reserve the role of heroine for myself?).

I sometimes think I was a creation of my father's imagination. Everything he could not allow himself to be, he let me be. When I came along, he already had his perfect family: two good-looking boys followed by two pretty girls, all bright and healthy. I was odd-looking anyway with my huge, honest eyes and angry, flaring nostrils. With me, he let go. He let me be outspoken and independent.

CHAPTER SEVEN

Fasting for my Father ❋ *Lighting up for Diwali*
An Opulent Dining Room ❋ *Chewing the Bones*
Bookworms ❋ *A Role Model*

When we came home from our convent school, we put our holy pictures aside and reverted to being a simple Hindu family. If it was Karvachauth, the fourth day of the waning moon in autumn, we knew my mother would be fasting for the health and longevity of my father and would not eat until the moon showed its face in the dark sky. She did this every year, as did all the married women we knew, though why my mother was obliged to pray for my father and my father never felt the need to pray for her remained perplexing. The ritual was carved in stone and never varied.

At night we all slept in a row on the verandah that faced the rose and jasmine garden. Even though our beds were next to each other, we were really quite isolated as each bed was enshrouded by a large, white mosquito net held up by four bamboo poles. My father slept at one end, with my mother next to him, then my baby sister, then me and my two older sisters.

Since married women were supposed to begin their fast at sunrise, my mother would set the alarm for four o'clock in the morning. This would allow her to get a quick bite to eat before the official fast began. The alarm would disturb my father, who would twist and turn and pull the quilt over his head.

My mother would emerge from her mosquito net, awaken any of her daughters who had so requested (Lalit, Kamal and me) and begin to brush her teeth vigorously with a twig from a neem tree. We would then all tiptoe to the pantry. Here my mother would take out *labdharay aloo* and *pooris* (sauced, spicy potatoes and deep-fried, puffed breads) from the warming oven and begin to eat. We sisters sat and watched. Every now and then, Bauwa would pop a bit of food from her plate into our mouths. Perhaps at that witching hour, when it was neither night nor day, my mother was quietly passing on an ancient tradition from her generation to ours.

Eventually we dressed and went to school and never said a word about what was happening at home. Even though I felt like shouting out, 'My mother is fasting for my father today so he won't die,' I said nothing. It was understood that what happened at home and what happened at school were unconnected. I had no school friends. I did play with and talk to many of the children, including Nash Engineer, a Parsi boy who was sweet and clever at arithmetic, but I never saw him or any other student outside the school. Our only real friends were our cousins in Delhi.

That evening my mother and the girls would go into the storeroom where, in the prayer section, mats had been laid down, oil lamps burned, fresh flowers poked out of brass vases and the 'holy food', *puas* (sweet, whole-wheat dumplings, rather like Italian zeppoles), were heaped on the lids of spouted, terracotta *karva* pots. We sat down, cross-legged, on the mats and began praying for my father. My father, meanwhile, smoked, read the paper and listened to the BBC.

Dadaji was much less distant at Diwali, the festival of lights, which also happened to be the Indian New Year. He did not participate much in the prayer part – he left that to my mother – but the lighting, the beautifying of the house and the parties were right up his alley. Here was a Hindu festival that demanded – not suggested but demanded – that the house be cleaned, painted and lit up, and that its owners open the doors wide, party and gamble so that the bright lights, gaiety and clinking of money might entice Lakshmi, the Goddess of Wealth, to visit and perhaps stay.

The scraping of old paint would start a good six weeks before Diwali. My father's planning would start much earlier. Each and every one of his friends had dressy Diwali dinners preceded and followed by gambling. No-one gambled during the rest of the year but Diwali was, well, Diwali. As the dinners went on for a whole month and were held every day except Diwali day when celebrations were family affairs, dates had to be cross-checked and invitations handwritten, envelopes licked shut and posted to friendly addresses all around Kanpur.

My father's lighting designs for his house were like no-one else's. Our neighbours opted for electric lights, large and small, running around their doors and bushes but this would have been too common for my father. He believed only in oil lamps and candles: candles on the verandahs and oil lamps outside where a few drips wouldn't make a mess. Oil lamps lined the roof and every parapet. My father also had railings of rough wooden branches built around the gardens, onto which dollops of wet clay were put at four-inch intervals. Small terracotta oil lamps were pressed into the clay and allowed to dry in place. On Diwali day, oil was poured into the lamps from long-spouted jugs, and wicks we had all helped make out of cotton wool were dropped into the centre of each lamp.

Prayers began at dusk and, as soon as they were over, the first oil lamps were lit in the prayer room. We would rush out with these and use them to start lighting all the candles and lamps. Soon the whole house would be glowing. My father would set off rockets and the children would be handed sparklers. Round and round I would spin with my sparkler until the house and I felt like one big ball of glitter.

Just before Veena was born, Dadaji decided he would not just paint the house but enlarge it to almost double its size. He would add an inner courtyard, two bathrooms, a new bedroom, a dressing room for his wife, a study for his girls, a dining room, a pantry, a storeroom and a long back verandah that aped the one at Number 7 in Delhi.

He consulted my eldest sister, Lalit, about the study. What colour would she want it? After poring over colour charts, she came up with mauve. For the moulding, she suggested gold. And why not? We probably had the only mauve and gold study in India, with a desk and chair made to my father's specifications.

Dadaji got even bolder with the dining room. He was a grand designer at heart, saddled in this life with a *ghee* factory. The dining room was large and rectangular, about thirty feet in length. First he had the walls covered with thick plaster. Then, while the plaster was still wet, he had the workmen go in with stiff, round brushes, stick them into the thick plaster and twist them slightly to form rosettes. Once the plaster dried, he had the walls painted a bright salmon pink. While his friends held back their dismay, he fearlessly went further and had the painters spray the rosettes whimsically with uneven showers of gold. We were glued to the daily developments in the dining room, unable to tear ourselves away once we returned from school. There was a fireplace as well and all the lighting fixtures were Art Deco. We were so proud.

My father ran all manner of contests there to teach us table manners. One of them was aimed at keeping our starched white damask napkins as clean as possible. The *dhobi* (laundryman) came once a week and the napkins had to last us for seven days. As our breakfasts were generally Western, the napkins fared pretty well except for the occasional bit of egg yolk. Lunches were Indian, and on weekdays we ate them in school. Dinners were often a mixture of what we called 'English' food and Indian food. We might start off with soup, such as a tomato soup made with our overabundant produce, and served with slices of bread, nicely crisped in the oven. Then we would go on to an Indian course, such as *rogan josh* (goat with cardamom), beet curry, okra with onions and whole-wheat chapatis, ending with a freshly-made jam tart, which our cook prepared to perfection.

There were many places to slip up here. The napkins could pick up dabs of tomato from the soup course. With the Indian course we were in really dangerous territory. We ate this course with our hands, naturally. My father would put his meat, with its sauce in a *katori* (small metal bowl), all together on his plate. first he would eat the pieces of meat with his chapati. Then – and he really loved this combined flavour – he would ask for the bowl of beets and add some of the sauce from the beets to the meat sauce and scoop it all up with more chapati.

Naturally, I wanted to do what my father did. But there would be some slip-ups, and traces of beet sauce with the dreaded yellow turmeric would find their way to the napkin. My father and mother both lectured us: 'Only use the tips of your fingers to eat . . . You must not dirty more than the first digit . . .' We were offered finger bowls after the Indian course but we dunked once and then used our napkins. So my father started checking our napkins, and whoever had the cleanest napkin at the end of the week was declared the winner. Always anxious to win, I stopped using my napkin altogether. In emergencies, I used my dress. My father soon put a stop to that, but with another such vice he was a bit more encouraging.

This had to do with bones. It started one cold winter's day when we had just eaten a chicken curry for dinner. The chickens were always bought live and usually by my father. I remember going with him to the poultry market where the birds were kept in rope cages. While the poultry-man held on to the squawking chicken, my father's long fingers with their beautifully shaped nails would advance towards the bird, go through the feathers and begin prob-ing and prodding. He said he needed to feel their breasts to see if there was any meat on the bones. The chosen bird would ride back in the car with us, still squawking away. The slaughtering was done at home, near the grapevines. It was thought that the blood would make the grapes redder. Then the chicken was plucked and taken to the kitchen at the end of a long, covered walkway. My mother would go there in the early evening to 'start off' the cooking. She would stand there perspiring, her cotton saree tucked between her legs. She would take some of the seasonings already chopped or ground by the *masalchi* (spice-grinder, person) and throw them into the hot oil in the *pateela* (cooking pot). Cardamom, cinnamon, bay leaf and cloves would go in, then some sliced red onions and a ground mix-ture of onions, garlic and ginger. This would be stirred around with a sprinkling of water until it was all golden. Some freshly ground cumin, coriander and turmeric would follow. Not too much chilli powder was used as my father couldn't stomach very hot food. Then the chicken pieces, all cut and skinned, would be added and stirred and stirred. My mother always said that the secret of a good curry lay in browning the spices and meat to just the right degree. Then she would add water and salt and leave. Her job was done. She could bathe and get dressed for the evening. It was left to the cook to finish the chicken curry.

Needless to say, such lovingly made food tasted good to the last bone. I enjoyed all of the chicken but I loved the bones, and would suck and chew them until there was almost nothing left. On one particular day I was still chewing on a bone when everyone got up from the table to listen to the radio. I followed, bone in hand, still chewing. My mother gave me an angry look, commented on my bad manners and asked me to return to the dining room and leave the bone on my plate. I was considering complying when my father came in with, 'Let her chew on the bone. She probably needs it.' And from that day on, I was allowed to chew on bones until they were reduced, in the case of chicken at least, to smithereens.

Marrow bones from a goat curry were another matter. Flavoured with cumin, coriander, onions and ginger, with the dark marrow popping up, they were glorious and we all wanted them. My parents had bought two sleek, silver marrow spoons to take the marrow out, but there were never enough marrow bones to go around. We just had to take turns: 'You had the marrow bone yesterday so it's MY turn today.'

All of us sisters liked to read. We could be caught all over the house in the weirdest positions: legs flung over the back of a wicker chair, book on chest; lying flat on the *takht* (divan) on our stomachs, the book on floor; head down on the desk, the book an inch from our eyes. Sometimes we read in the garden. As it got darker, my mother would ask us to come in. Lalit and Kamal listened. I went on reading until Bauwa yelled, 'If you go on reading in the dark you will end up with glasses.'

Eventually, my eyes were checked. Sure enough, I needed glasses. Another woe! I would never be a pretty girl. Meanwhile, my sisters, already dainty and lovely teenagers, pranced around in their new, multicoloured, wedge-heel shoes!

Around this time my parents became very friendly with a doctor. She was always referred to as a 'lady-doctor' and was the only respectable female I knew who worked. I immediately resolved to be a doctor. I followed Dr Chandrakanta around whenever she visited, admiring her firm manner, her large watch, her sanitized smell and her simple handloom sarees. She was not married as all the women around me were, and had a clear sense of mission. I so desperately wanted to be her.

CHAPTER EIGHT

My Caring, Reticent Sister ❋ The Useful Club
The Death of a Cousin

As we girls got older, the responsibility for our general welfare fell more and more on Lalit. It started with homework and crept up from there. My mother could hardly help us with school work as it was all in English. Lalit had already gone over what Kamal and I were studying so we naturally turned to her. Her own nature also pushed her to help us out. She began to choose the patterns for our dresses and coats; she remembered our birthdays; and at Easter, she made sure I got a prettily decorated Easter egg from the Goan bakers at Valerio's as she knew that would make me giddy with joy.

Once, when we were all playing on a high pile of rolled-up winter quilts, my youngest sister, Veena, tumbled down and broke her arm. It was Lalit who held her and telephoned my parents who were away at a dinner party.

Perhaps because of this responsibility for her sisters' wellbeing, and because she was a teenager in a walled compound, Lalit began disappearing into herself, into some inner recesses where I could not always follow her. When she spoke, if the subject was anything other than of an intellectual or household nature, I felt that more was left unsaid than said. I was so used to unburdening myself of every last emotion that, as I got older, I began noticing her reticence more and more. I remember years later asking her in some desperation, 'But what are you feeling? What are you FEELING?' She had learnt to keep her feelings to herself. She never stopped being a very caring, loving older sister to me. She listened to every last outburst of mine through the years, calming and soothing me, but her own heart remained private.

And then a cousin died. This was the first death in our joint family and it left me desolate. I was about seven years old.

As we moved seamlessly from Kanpur to Delhi, we would take up with the cousins of similar ages to us as soon as we got there. The cousin closest in age to me was Brijesh, the third son of my father's youngest sister, Kiran Bhua. We would climb trees together, eat *chaat* (spicy snacks) and go for walks to the Yamuna River, hand in hand. I even started dressing like him, in boy's shorts. Best of all, we had started a club together.

A few years earlier, when we were both sitting under the stairs that led to the roof of Number 7, we decided to cement our friendship by forming a very private club with just two members, him and me.

'What would the club do?' I wondered.

'Well, it could collect something,' Brijesh ventured. He had a fine nose, thin, well-shaped lips and thick dark hair.

What might we collect that mattered deeply to us? The answer was clear. It would have to be stationery. We both loved stationery. Special stationery. And so began the collection of The Useful Club (which I have to this day) – pens that could write in six colours, matching sets of silver pads and pencils for keeping bridge scores (all the cousins played bridge, starting around the age of six), pencils with tassels, boxed gold pencils, sleek wooden rulers, erasers that looked like toffee . . . It was decided that I would be in charge of this collection and that it would be housed in the large bottom drawer of a cupboard my mother kept in our Kanpur bedroom. Of course, whenever I visited Delhi for the holidays, I would bring the collection with me so we could examine it and add to it.

Lalit went on a trip to Delhi, with my father I think. The rest of us stayed behind in Kanpur. This is the story she told on her return, and it is permanently etched in my head.

It was the afternoon of a very hot day and most of the household in Delhi was napping. She was sitting alone on the long front verandah when she noticed a stray dog with a strange gait meandering down the front drive. The next thing she remembered was hearing screaming and sounds of a struggle. She ran through the opening in the henna hedge into the south courtyard. There, in front of my middle uncle, Shibbudada's, bedroom was the dog, growling, frothing at the mouth and clutching Brijesh's hand. She tried to shake the hand free but the dog's teeth were firmly embedded around Brijesh's thumb so it took a while. Meanwhile she yelled for help but not before getting a lot of blood on herself as well. Family and servants came running and the dog was ultimately captured for examination in case it had rabies.

Lalit and my father left for Kanpur. It was in Kanpur that we got the call from Delhi saying that the dog did have rabies, that Brijesh was getting his rabies injections and that Lalit should get them too.

Lalit got her shots at the hospital on the way to school. I would go in with her. She would have to lie down and expose her stomach. The biggest, thickest needle would be poked slowly right into her soft belly. The medicine went in slowly too. Her face expressed her agony but she did not make a sound. I wanted to cry for her but did not dare. It seemed to take forever. I would think of Brijesh too. He was so much younger. The same would be happening to him.

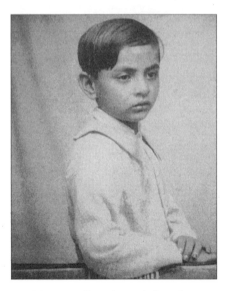

My cousin Brijesh, aged about four.

Some months later we learned that Brijesh had rabies and that he was in hospital. The injections had not worked for him. It happened sometimes, they said. We got daily reports from Delhi. It was an agonizing death, they said, complete with hydrophobia and all the havoc that rabies wreaks. He cried for water but could not swallow a single drop.

CHAPTER NINE

Divided Loyalties ✳ *Preparing for War* ✳ *Film Buffs*
The Nazi Connection ✳ *Wolfie and the Grey Horse*
The End of the Kanpur Idyll

World War II was in full swing and it was testing loyalties. My father's ambivalences were seeping into all of us. We trusted our father enough to want to think like him but what was he thinking?

First of all, there was the British Army in Europe, fighting the Nazis. Thousands of Indians were fighting along with them and were dying daily, just as they had done in World War I. We would get the reports: so-and-so's son was killed in Italy; so-and-so's brother was killed in Turkey. This was not in the British press. We just heard it. Indians were dying for the British while we, as a nation, were fighting the British in India for our independence. We were fighting non-violently, under the guidance of Mahatma Gandhi, but we were fighting nonetheless. We wanted the British to win in Europe but to be free of them in India.

The British Army was also in the jungles of Burma, skirmishing with the Japanese who were advancing towards India. Fighting along with them were 700,000 Indians, many of them Gurkhas, who were dying daily too. Now, in the same Burmese jungles, fighting *with* the Japanese and *against* the British, were Indians of the INA, the Indian National Army, whose leaders were such heart-throbs that when they were captured by the British and tried in Delhi's Red Fort, all teenage Indian girls cried their eyes out. The INA hoped to march into India with the Japanese and free the country.

Meanwhile, much of North India, and this included us, was preparing for war with air-raid drills and blackouts. We didn't know who was going to bomb us but we were ready. By the early 1940s our windows and skylights had black shades on them. My father had trenches dug all along one side of the house and we were fully prepared to dive in at the slightest hint of warfare from any quarter.

Life continued, however, and as a family we went to the cinema almost every week, partly to take our minds off the war. Although the name 'Bollywood' had yet to be invented, Bombay Talkies was a major studio of the time, and we managed to see every film it made, even its 'war-effort' films. Studios around the world were producing these films, each from their own national point of view. Bombay Talkies films were decidedly pro-British. We saw British, American and Indian war-effort films, or whatever was showing at the picture house. We were film buffs, with my father once declaring that 'Joan Crawford is a very handsome woman'. I didn't know until then that a woman could be called handsome.

In those days each film concluded with a recording of the national anthem, then *God Save the King*. Everyone was supposed to stand up as soon as the Union Jack waved on the screen. Well, after having seen the pro-British war-effort film and enjoying it, my father's form of protest against British rule was to walk out as soon as the flag appeared. His wife followed him, and the girls, like little ducklings, waddled behind them in support. Here, at least, we had devised a clear procedure to follow.

A much more serious issue was my father's cousin and dear friend, Guru Chacha. Guru Chacha had gone to Germany to study. There he had fallen in love with and married a German girl, Toni Aunty. As the drum roll for the war began, Guru Chacha took to the German airwaves, on the Nazi side.

My poor father was appalled. He glued himself to his large Phillips radio, hand on dial. There would be electronic whining and static and then my uncle's voice would come forth, as clear and sharp as ever. 'Guru is on, Guru is on,' my father would cry hysterically. We would all come running. My mother would make sure that my father had a cup of tea or a whisky in hand to calm him down. We listened to Guru Chacha and then to the BBC, talking of the same war.

I remember Guru Chacha and Toni Aunty returning to India after the war and Indian independence. Guru Chacha had put all his savings into a large machine he was convinced would make him a fortune in the new India. It was a doughnut machine.

Poor, lost Guru Chacha. Independent India, however sweet-toothed, did not take kindly to doughnuts and his venture proved quite ruinous. The last I heard, he and Toni Aunty had turned to some Indian religious group for solace and peace.

During the war years, we also acquired some unusual protection in the shape of a dog. My mother had, until then, clung to the old Hindu school of thought that all animals were dirty, germ-carrying creatures that should be kept outside the house. She was not prepared for Wolfie. A German shepherd, Wolfie was not, strictly, ours. His original German master, Karl Schneider, had come to work in my father's factory as a chemist but once the war started, he was interned and I never saw him again. Before he was carted off, he begged my father to take care of Wolfie. My father begged my mother and she ultimately relented. And so we got our first dog.

The war also brought us a horse, a dappled grey and white beauty I loved. We could no longer go to school in our car as petrol was strictly rationed. My father hired a tonga – a very simple horse-drawn carriage – to take us back and forth. The horse that came with this carriage had an inexplicable tendency to fall down and lie prone on the road, at the oddest moments. This would leave the carriage high in the air with three girls in pigtails screaming their heads off. My father soon tired of this arrangement. He bought his own horse and a fancy, high-off-the-ground, red tonga. It came with an equally fancy tinkle-tinkle bell in the front that the turbaned coachman could depress with his foot. The stables, where my adored grey horse could rest on straw, were near my father's office so it gave me another destination to walk to every day as I did the rounds of the gardens. After every tonga ride, the horse needed to be walked. I walked along with him as I admired my father who, with his horse and tonga, seemed to me the most stylish man in the world.

Our cocooned idyll in Kanpur, such as it was, came to an abrupt end in 1944 when my father decided to leave his job and return to Delhi.

The pull of Delhi, with my grandfather tugging at the strings, had been constant. Now Babaji was getting really old and my father's guilt was mounting. There were probably other triggers but

I never really understood them. All I know is that the announcement seemed sudden and my mother was heartbroken. She cried almost constantly for a month. We would go to visit my parents' friends for farewell parties and my mother would end up in floods of tears. My father seemed distracted, as if his eyes were confronting a hundred ghosts. Both my parents seemed to know that perhaps the best, most independent part of their lives was coming to an end. Henceforth, they would be mere cogs in a joint family machine controlled by other, more domineering figures.

Schooling, that constant problem, was a consideration again. While my parents, my baby sister and I would be joining my brothers after eight years of on-off companionship, we would be leaving my two older sisters behind. They were to start boarding school in Kanpur, and after two years transfer to another boarding school – a sister convent – in Nainital, a Himalayan hill station beside a lake.

My father did wrest one concession from my grandfather. We would have our own house. No, not in New Delhi, a respectable distance away as my father had wanted, but just across the street, on the inner corner of the same road named after my grandfather. Number 5 was a much smaller, more rough-and-ready house, one of two my grandfather had built as rental properties. We could live there, but we still had to eat all our main meals in Number 7.

CHAPTER TEN

Spellbinding Shibbudada ❈ *Two Tragic Marriages*
Sadness and a Conspiracy of Silence

D uring the eight years we were in Kanpur, family life in
Delhi had continued apace but with an entirely different
flavour.

If there was one man in our joint family around whom the earth
revolved it was Shibbudada, my father's middle brother who lived at
Number 7. If he smiled at you, you swelled with confidence and
security. If he ignored you or looked down on you, you withered on
the vine. Some invariably fared better than others. We all felt only as
good as the benediction he bestowed on us.

As an infant, Shibbudada had suffered a strange accident. My
grandmother, Bari Bauwa, was transporting him from one town to
another in a bullock cart and had fallen asleep, holding him in her
arms. As her grip loosened slightly, one of the baby's feet that had
been dangling outside the cart began scraping against a wheel. Over
the course of the journey, most of his arch got rubbed away. He
healed, but was saddled with one oddly shaped foot.

He was not as tall or as good looking as my father or his eldest
brother, Chand, the tallest of them all who was an engineer by
profession, and generally away in the eastern states of Orissa and
Bihar. In Shibbudada's case it was his stage-managed vivacity and
ebullience that endeared him to most of our world.

[65]

He had grown up to be his mother's darling, indeed the darling of his brothers and sisters and the whole town. He wooed those he favoured with overly generous gestures and a determined intensity, charming them with his deep and genuine passion for Indian classical music, Persian and Urdu poetry, and his well-honed skills as a raconteur. He could hold you spellbound.

As a young man he had come across a beautiful, delicately framed Kayastha girl and fallen passionately in love with her. I never met her or saw any photographs of her but could well imagine what she might have looked like. My uncle, tidal force that he was, continually made plans to bind her family to ours by arranging marriages between her relatives and members of our family. Her youngest sister married a cousin, and her niece is married to my eldest brother, both marriages arranged courtesy of Shibbudada.

He was determined to marry his love but there was the slight matter of the horoscopes. They did not match. Priests were cajoled but they would not budge. They predicted, not the usual, vague 'seven years of bad luck' but a disastrous marriage ending in a quick death of the bride.

Shibbudada was too deeply in love and unstoppable. The marriage took place and, six months later, the bride died of typhoid. Shibbudada was still a young man and, after the few years allowed for mourning, his family began suggesting that he marry again. He kept saying no. They kept asking until they wore him down and he told them to go ahead and arrange it.

In those days marriages were nearly always arranged with the bride's side sending offers to the families of eligible young men. Shibbudada, a very successful lawyer, was highly eligible, and marriage offers were pouring in. One offer from a family in Agra looked promising and my aunts – my father's sisters – were sent on

Shibbudada at one of the three-legged races he organized. He stands in the centre, attached to Kamal. I am to his left, attached to Brijesh. Raghudada, in white shirt and glasses, is tied to his sister Sheila.

the delicate mission of checking out the young lady in question. They so wanted to get it right and make their adored brother happy again.

The story gets a bit hazy here. This is the version provided by an eyewitness, my aunt, Saran Bhua (my father's second-youngest sister). She and some of her sisters were asked to go to a house in the Old City of Agra and to climb the stairs to the roof. The possible bride-to-be would be on an adjacent roof, or on a roof just across a narrow lane (there is some confusion here) and available for viewing. The possible bride-to-be appeared and was dazzling. According to my aunt, dusk was approaching, the sun was just setting behind the girl and perhaps their eyes deceived them. Or were they deliberately tricked by the old bait-and-switch trick? No-one dared assign any blame as it could have fallen anywhere.

Throughout the wedding ceremony the bride had her face covered by her *ghoongat* (veil), as was customary. When the *ghoongat* was lifted, it revealed a decidedly plain woman. It did not reveal the wit and intelligence the woman possessed in plenty, but whatever he saw, it was enough for my poetry-spouting, beauty-loving middle uncle to hate her for life.

He hated her enough to shift to his own, separate quarters. His wife, Taiji, was left to find solace in the middle room between our northeast room in Number 7 and my grandfather's southeast room. My middle uncle, meanwhile, lived in the annexe across the south courtyard. He hated her but still had four children with her, one of them a hare-lipped baby neither of them could stomach. My dear, soft-hearted mother breast-fed this baby until he died.

Shibbudada's children, who seemed initially to take after their mother, did not appeal to him. He ignored them. It was as if they didn't exist. In a joint family, this was both hard to do and easy to do. As Shibbudada was the self-designated Pied Piper for the family's young hordes, he could be arranging fun and games for all of them while actually bestowing his loving glances on just a chosen few. Like a magician drawing a rabbit from a hat, he did magical deeds for all the children, eliciting from them whoops of delight.

Nothing excited me more than an announcement by Shibbudada that he had asked the *khomcha-wallah* over for our Saturday tea. That was akin to telling a Western child that he could have a whole sweet shop for the entire afternoon.

A *khomcha-wallah*, as it happened, had nothing sweet to offer. His normal habitat was the street, usually busy thoroughfares. Here he would wander eternally, or so it seemed to me, a basket balanced on his sturdy head, a cane stool tucked into the crook of his free arm. Whenever the crowd seemed promising, he set his stool down, lowered his basket to rest on it, and then began hawking his wares.

The basket was a mini-shop, containing a category of food

*Pied Piper-like, Shibbudada gathers together his own children
and many of us cousins in the lovingly cultivated garden of Number 7.
I am hiding behind the chrysanthemums, busily chatting.*

unknown in the West – hot, sour and savoury snacks known
through much of north India as *chaat*. The food was half-prepared,
and many permutations – of ingredients, seasonings, sauces and
dressings – were possible. If one asked, say, for *dahi baras*, the
khomcha-wallah would take split pea patties (they had already been
fried and soaked in warm water, which also got rid of their oiliness)
and put them on a 'plate' of semi-dried leaves. Then he took some
plain yoghurt beaten to a creamy consistency, and spread it over the

top. Over the yoghurt went the salt and one or more of the yellow, red or black spice mixtures that sat in wide bowls. Those who wanted a mild, cumin-black pepper-dried mango flavour got only the black mixture. Those who said gleefully, as I did, 'make it very hot', also got the yellow and red mixtures filled with several varieties of chillies. If we had an extra craving for a sweet-and-sour taste, we would ask for a tamarind chutney. A wooden spoon would ·disappear into the depths of a brown sauce, as thick as melted chocolate. It would emerge only to drop a dark, satiny swirl over our *dahi baras*. As we ate them, the *dahi baras* would melt in our mouths with the minimum of resistance, the hot spices would bring tears to our eyes, the yoghurt would cool us down, and the tamarind would perk up our taste buds as nothing else could. This to us was heaven.

It was a taste of heaven with many emotional ifs and buts. We would watch our three cousins, Shibbudada's two sons and daughter, jumping around in general glee with the rest of us, but every now and then they would throw a quick glance at their father, their large dark eyes begging for another kind of crumb. Perhaps a hug, a touch of the hand. They never got it. The worst part was that we were all Shibbudada's unwitting accomplices. Because he made himself indispensable, we all wanted a piece of the Pied Piper. The children joined what the elders – perhaps ridden with the responsibility of having arranged the match – had already established: a conspiracy of silence on the subject of Shibbudada's behaviour towards his family. The *chaat* was heavenly for sure, but the aftertaste was slightly bitter.

Every now and then Taiji, Shibbudada's wife, would send one of her children to their father to ask for something they needed. It was, at times, just her desperate way of trying to reach him. She seemed to love him and want him to the end. The child would stand uncomfortably, like a stranger, at his annexe door. Sometimes the child would be asked in and sometimes there would be a summary dismissal.

From a very young age, I lived with this constant possibility of emotional havoc. After every such destabilizing incident, I would need to bury my head in my mother's starchy saree or my father's tweedy coat. Most of the time, however, my father was not there. Before we moved to Delhi, he would travel with us on the train to drop us off, say *salaam* to all, and return to his work in Kanpur. Besides, Shibbudada was his worshipped, god-like older brother. Dadaji never, *ever* questioned him. My mother's position on the joint family totem pole was lowly. She was the youngest daughter-in-law in a household where the only women who were expansively comfortable were my all-powerful grandmother and her visiting daughters. This was not my unassertive mother's turf. She merely watched, felt a lot but was too restrained to speak. I could not say anything either. I had to learn to live as if these traumas were not happening at all.

CHAPTER ELEVEN

My Gang ❋ *Fishing, Shooting and Swimming*
The Watermelon Fields ❋ *Piercing Screams*

My cousin Rajesh – the one who rushed for his air gun after my toast was snatched away by the kite – was Shibbudada's youngest son. He was just a little bit older than me and, as he always lived in Delhi, I spent nearly all my time with him whenever I was there, especially after Brijesh's death. I also played with other visiting cousins my age, all of whom happened to be boys. Mahesh, with his soft greenish-brown eyes, was the eldest in our gang. The son of my father's youngest sister, Kiran Bhua, he would grow up to be a prominent nuclear scientist. Then there was Lovy (Ravi, actually), my aunt Saran Bhua's oldest, who was to become a geologist, and his younger brother Shashi, who seemed to resemble my strapping grandfather in old photographs I had seen. There was Suresh, the youngest son of my third aunt, Prem Bhua, and of course Rajesh. This was my gang.

It was Rajesh who taught me how to fish and shoot and swim. These were, supposedly, boys' activities but as I hung around only with boy cousins – the girl cousins and my sisters being much older – I seemed destined for the periphery. I could watch the boys play cricket and sometimes, as an indulgence, be allowed to bowl underhand or even bat. But when the boys had their matches, I could only watch.

*A family group gathers for a formal portrait, complete with couch,
on a picnic in about 1940. My grandparents sit in the centre. I am in the front row
with my 'gang' (left to right): Suresh, Lovy, me, Rajesh, Mahesh and Shashi.
A turbaned bearer stands top right, waiting on us all.*

While I was still little, fishing too was out of my reach. It seemed
to be an exotic male ritual in which I could play no part. Oh yes, I
could stand around as the boys went under the *ber* (jujube) tree to
dig for their earthworms. I was not allowed to dig them up myself.
I could watch them attach lead weights to their fishing lines to make
them sink, and pieces of cane to make them float. But when I said,
'I can do that,' no-one listened.

One year, when I was five, all this changed, thanks to Rajesh.
'May I come with you this time, please?' I asked him.

'No,' was his initial reply.

The Yamuna River was just across the street below us. Our little
world was considered quite safe for children to wander about in, as

long as we did not actually go into the water. The boys would pack their gear and off they would go whenever the sun relented.

'Why?' I had persisted.

'Because you are a girl.'

I hated being unfairly limited. 'But I can do everything you can.'

'No you can't. Why did you scream so much yesterday when we were digging up earthworms?'

'Because you cut an earthworm in half with your spade and both halves were wriggling.'

'The boys didn't scream.'

'I'll get used to it. Please let me come fishing with you.'

In the end he relented and I donned my boy's shorts. Rajesh even threaded a worm on my hook for me, and when I caught my first fish – a freshwater eel so snakelike that I dropped my rod and ran in fear – he put his arm around me and calmed me down. It would be easier the next time, he said.

It was Rajesh who taught me to shoot as well. Since I could fish, perhaps I could shoot too. 'Hold the gun up. Higher, higher. Now close one eye. No, not that eye, silly, the other one. *Arey* . . . that . . . wasn't . . . bad.' It turned out that I was 'not a bad' shot.

We approached swimming in quite another way. When winter winds blowing down from the northern Himalayas gave way to hot desert blasts from the south, we had three months to go into the river before the monsoon rains made its waters rage and rise. Morning, before breakfast, was the best time. We would roll our bathing suits into our towels and start walking.

In the early years, when we were still small and threatening to go into the water, not just fish on its edges, the women came along. Sometimes it was Shibbudada who took us. Later, an older cousin was considered adequate.

We were all quite familiar with the two miles or so of the Yamuna that meandered just beyond our house. After all, we had grown up there and developed a proprietary passion for that stretch of sand, scrub and water. We had charted every detail of its topography, felt it with our feet. *Our* patch of the river started to the north with the Bund, a stone embankment that tried, quite fruitlessly, to prevent the river from flooding in our direction during the monsoon season, and ended, south of our house, with a small temple that had steps leading down to the water. Between the Bund and the temple were stretches of sand and rock we felt we owned.

It seemed to be the tradition in Delhi that while the men and boys could swim in the river, the women and girls could only bathe and 'dip'. When the women came with us, they wore their sarees, soft summer greens, pinks and yellows. They would take off their *chappals* as soon as they hit the sand and then walk into the river fully clothed. Here they would sit down in the water, their heads disappearing beneath the gentle waves. All that could be seen were their sarees billowing and puffing up around them. This was a 'dip' and about as far as the women went. They would take one, two or three dips. If the day was really hot they might sit around in the water for a while and then just walk out, their sarees clinging to their plump, voluptuous bodies. All this time the boys swam and the girls splashed about.

There was no formal place for ladies to undress and it was not expected. Centuries of custom had taught the women to improvise individual tents around themselves with their fresh, dry sarees. Inside this hand-held enclosure, they could slip out of their wet clothes, their modesty fully guarded. Moving arms, elbows, legs and knees kept the outlines of the tents in constant motion. Heads would emerge, followed by arms and clad torsos. Soon the dry sarees, having performed their changing room functions, would be wound around the body – once, twice and, with a flick of the hand, the heavily embroidered ends would be flung over their left shoulders.

The wet hair would be unwound. The ladies would then bend their bodies forward so their hair would fall over their faces and almost touch the ground. With towels stretched between two hands, the wetness would be beaten out and the hair flung back again. Then the call would come, 'Out of the water. Time to go home.' After a brief stop at the temple to have cooling sandalwood paste smeared on our foreheads, the group would amble back.

I knew I would never be content with 'dips' so I turned again to my cousin Rajesh. He had studied swimming at Modern School, the same school my brothers had attended. He streaked through the water like a torpedo and I wanted to do the same.

We started with the watermelon.

As indoor ceiling fans barely made a dent in the relentless summer heat, we were all driven out of our rooms to sleep on the front lawn. Twenty or so beds would be lined up between the jujube tree and the hedge near the tamarind tree in two or three rows, gauzy rectangular containers, each holding a prone body. The first rays of the sun and the incessant chattering of birds would bring the prone bodies to life. Most summer mornings, we would lie in our beds and talk to each other through the mosquito netting. We would begin making plans for the day. 'Let's go and get a watermelon,' a cousin would suggest. Someone's mother, overhearing us from another row of beds, would add, 'Take Jai Singh with you. He will help you carry it back.'

Jai Singh was Shibbudada's personal manservant whose accrued status resulted directly from the special status of his master. Because Shibbudada's say carried weight, so did Jai Singh's. Like most of our servants, he was from 'the hills', a British euphemism for the Himalayas. The highest mountains in the world had, scattered across them, thousands of small, picturesque but impoverished villages where farmers' children walked barefoot in the snow and families kept warm in winter by huddling on the floor just above their animals. Some family members stayed behind to tend the fields but most of the young men came down in droves looking for work on 'the plains'.

Many of them worked for us and were housed in a long row of servants' quarters that ran west from the tamarind tree. Jai Singh was one of them. A fine-looking man with a chiselled nose and small, piercing eyes that saw everything. He could, had he been educated, been a leader of men. In his present situation, he was shrewd and calculating and a possessor of many family secrets. Once, when he was escorting us to the river and I jumped off a rock onto a jagged piece of glass, he ran all the way home with me in his arms. As I bled and cried, he tried to amuse me by imitating my lisp. Although I was only about three at the time, I have a clear image of Jai Singh's face, smelling of the *bidis* (small cheroots) he smoked, bending down and laughing at me as he ran up the steep road that curved around to the front of Number 7, and teasing me with, 'Say *khirki* [window] again. You can't say it now, can you? Okay, say it your way, *khilki*. Who says *khilki*, huh?'

With Jai Singh as escort, we had gone down to the river for a watermelon that day, when I was about five. Across the river from the Bund, up beyond a sandy embankment, were the watermelon fields. He stayed on the near shore with our clothes while we donned our bathing suits and waited for the boat.

This was a ferryboat, a big, rough, wooden, handmade creation used mostly by the milkmen and farmers who brought their produce to the city for sale. The ferryman stood high up at one end and used a pole to guide the boat across the river.

We were hoisted up and taken slowly across the calm waters. This was the river's summer guise. During the monsoons it could rise and lash savagely at our cellar gates. On the other side of the Yamuna, we jumped down on our own, chased each other up the sandy embankment and made a run for the watermelon fields.

The watermelons seemed to grow right out of the sand. There they were, dozens and dozens of monstrous green balls, barely acknowledging the withered, browning vines they were attached to, just lying there asking to be taken away from the burning sun and devoured.

We chose one, paid the farmer for it and rolled it down the embankment to the edge of the water.

'Now,' said Rajesh, 'I will teach you how to swim.'

He pushed the watermelon into the river. The giant fruit began to float. 'Jump in after it and grab it with your hands,' he instructed. 'Keep your arms stretched and your head down. Kick your feet without bending your knees.'

'I'll drown, I'll drown. The water is so deep in the middle of the river.'

'No you won't drown. We are all with you.'

And so, with my cousins flanking me on all sides, I crossed the Yamuna with the help of a watermelon. It was my first swimming lesson.

Jai Singh scooped me up on the other side. He threw towels on all our shoulders and carried the watermelon triumphantly home where it was cut up and demolished. My grandmother pickled the rind. No signs of the fruit were left except the seeds, which were put in the sun and left to dry for future use.

It was during one of our summer trips to Delhi that I had my ears pierced. My finicky father would never consent to one of the traditional women who came to the house and pierced ears with small gold hoops. They had done it all their lives but my father insisted that they were untrained and unhygienic. He wanted us to go to a proper doctor who would use 'clean instruments'. My father marched all of us girls off to Dr S.B. Mathur, the family physician, whose office was in Chandni Chowk, the heart of the Old City, and who knew as much about piercing ears as he did about existentialism.

The doctor took a deep, brave breath. He carefully sterilized some needles and thread, dabbed our ears with antiseptic lotion and shoved the fat needle and thick thread in. As might be expected, each of us screamed in turn as our ears were violated.

When we went home, with the ugly knotted thread loops dangling from our ears, my mother and grandmother immediately fell upon us with home remedies for 'quick' healing. In a process that went on three times a day for a month, *ghee* (clarified butter) was heated in a *katori* (small metal bowl) with ground turmeric. The *ghee* turned a bright yellow colour but the aroma, I remember, was pleasingly earthy. Sticks, taken from a clean broom, were covered at one end with cotton wool, dipped into the boiling liquid and the bright colour transferred to our ears under the guise of a hot fomentation. Turmeric was considered the best antiseptic that the heavens had provided. That it left an indelible stain seemed to bother no-one. For one month we went to school with cooked, yellow earlobes, drawing the stares of all our schoolmates. My ears were so badly and unevenly pierced that I can barely wear earrings today.

CHAPTER TWELVE

The Drawing Room ❦ *Winter Evenings: Family, Friends,*
Lemonade, Nuts and Pakoris ❦ *Dining at the Long Tables*

O n winter evenings in Delhi, we all gathered in the drawing
room where Ishri, my grandfather's manservant, had
already lit a fire. 'It must have snowed in Simla,' we
would say, rubbing our cold hands and pulling shawls, cardigans and
coats closer to ourselves. Simla, that much-loved Himalayan hill
town where my sister Kamal had been born, was in the very distant
north, but whenever it snowed there, icy blasts made sure we got the
news.

No-one in the Number 7 household had been blessed with
much sense of style so furniture, bought wholesale at auction, was
shoved against all four walls. As you entered the drawing room from
the gallery end, there was the radio around which we huddled to
hear Hindi movie songs at midday and cricket commentaries in the
afternoons. Beyond it, on the same north side, was a big sofa, above
which hung a large framed print of Hope sitting, head bent, on top
of the globe, playing a lyre. In the corner was a kind of piano that
could only be played by pumping wind into it with a pair of foot
pedals. Then, as you turned the corner to the east side, there were
overstuffed chairs galore of disparate designs. Above them on the
wall, attempting to give the room some cohesion, was a tinted,
rather nicely framed photograph of my grandfather, looking quite

*Cousins Rajesh (left, here in my grandfather's favourite seat)
and Suresh in the drawing room at Number 7.*

Edwardian – Raj Narain, Barrister-at-law. Next, on a stand and
enclosed in glass, was a miniature marble reproduction of the Taj
Mahal and a potted palm on a stand. On the south side, the fireplace
held a rather lovely Chinese cloisonné urn with dragons. On the
mantelpiece was a print of a young, free-spirited lady (European but
with an Eastern abandon), gazing into a fish bowl.

Surrounding the fireplace was an upholstered bench. Farther
into the room was another large sofa where my grandfather sat and
more overstuffed chairs. There was a Persian carpet of exquisite
workmanship on the floor, which was also used as seating. The
drawing room was, basically, a functional room that had been
designed – or not designed – to hold a lot of people.

The evening routine in winter hardly varied unless there was a
religious festival, wedding or music recital.

As sunset gave way to dusk, the air slowly filled with the
perfumed smoke of *uppalas*, dried cow-dung cakes, being burned in
braziers throughout the city. This was, and to some extent still is,

the winter smell of Delhi. As the cows mostly ate hay, that was what their dung smelled like.

When the soft haze of the *uppala* smoke began drifting through the glow of the setting sun, squawking birds by the hundreds, propelled by their own clocks, would begin circling our trees in flocks: green-feathered parrots with red beaks, sparrows, yellow-beaked mynahs and also the dreaded crows. They would fly round and round above the mighty tamarind, the umbrella-shaped jujube, the mulberry near the gate, the medicinal neem and the mangoes. As they circled, they would come lower and lower, disappearing, as night fell, into the darkness of the foliage. You could still hear them for a while, though, chattering noisily, and then there would be quiet.

Ishri would light the fire in the fireplace then hobble off to prepare my grandfather's hookah, his hubble-bubble water pipe, a fairly formal, floor-standing version. I would follow Ishri because the odour of that wet, dark, manly-but-sweet tobacco drove me wild. Ishri would make a ball of the tobacco and deposit it in the top section, the *chillum*, of the hookah. Over this he would arrange small pieces of burning charcoal and blow on them repeatedly until they glowed, his cheeks puffing like a toad as he did so.

My white-bearded grandfather, supporting himself with his cane, would come through the door that connected his room to the drawing room and settle down in his accustomed place on the right side of the sofa. However old he may have been by this time, he was still king of the household. Ishri would put down the hookah and set a whisky and soda on a small table near it. Babaji would draw on the hookah. A roll of gurgling sounds would follow as the air went through the water in the pipe. He would then take a sip of his whisky. It was the start of another winter evening at Number 7.

The women, freshly washed and changed into their evening

sarees, would follow, coming in from various doors, one after the other. The first two were generally commandeered by my grand-father to sit at his feet on the Persian carpet and play chess, or more often *chaupar* (a form of Parcheesi), a game using three long, rectangular dice. He directed the game and the women played it, more to please him than each other.

The children, having finished their sports or their homework, wandered in as well. If we passed my grandfather, he would dip a finger in his glass of whisky and give us a lick. We were known to queue up for these licks. The men returning from work would start dribbling in as well. If Shibbudada happened to come through the door, which was rare as he was generally out at musical events, bridge parties or at Roshanara Club, the air in the room would immediately become supercharged. He nearly always came in demanding our immediate attention. 'Look what I have for you! These are dates from Iran. Sweet, sweet dates. Imbedded in each one of them are the best walnuts you can ever hope to eat. Take a bite. Just take a bite' Yells and shrieks of delight would follow. Taiji would look up at Shibbudada with fresh hope, forgetting for a moment the years of unfulfilled expectations.

This was the social part of our day and we never knew who might visit. No-one needed to call before showing up. Mostly it was relatives, both close and distant. There was no formality, only familiarity. Om and Shant, green-eyed sisters, and granddaughters of Babaji's younger brother next door, might walk over to regale us with their wit or impersonations. Prema and Krishna, from Number 10, the daughters of my father's eldest and most beautiful sister, Bhuaji, could stop by. Prema and Krishna were about Lalit's age and identical twins. One wore glasses, the other did not. They were born as triplets but only two had survived. I remember once,

Prema and Krishna arriving without Prema's customary glasses on. As we looked quizzically, they told us they had been to a guru who had given Prema special eye exercises to do at dawn every day while gazing at the rising sun. She had done the exercises religiously and now she was cured! She was indeed.

Other than the unassailable family rule that you always gave your chair to anyone older than you, seating was very much a grab-what-you-can arrangement. Generally, the grown-ups settled into all the plump sofas and upholstered chairs while we cousins draped ourselves where we could, on the arms of the sofas, the carpet and the bench by the fireplace.

All social occasions are fuelled with food and drink, and our winter evenings in the drawing room were no exception. The men were offered whisky sodas, the women tea, and the children squashes and lemonade. Squashes were fruit concentrates sold by the bottle. You poured some into a glass, added water and ice and you had a tolerable drink. I disliked squashes intensely. The Glacier brand we drank was manufactured in the Himalayan foothills by close family friends. My father had once wrested a superb marmalade recipe from them. Even that refused to endear these lifeless squashes to me. Now, lemonades were another matter.

In the mornings as we sat sunning ourselves in the front verandah, we would hear the sound of hooves and the cry of a hawker, 'Lemonade-wallah . . . Lemonade-wallah.' We would plead with our mothers to get some cases for the evening. A servant would be dispatched to the gate to signal to the lemonade-wallah that his wares were desired, and the lemonade-wallah, sitting atop his laden horse-cart, would come clip-clopping in.

Lemonades had nothing to do with lemons. They were carbonated drinks, sodas really, that came in special, to-be-returned glass bottles with marbles in their narrow necks. It was the marbles that held the fizz inside. Once the marble was pushed down with a stopper-shaped gadget, red, green or clear lemonade was there for the taking.

With the drinks were served the inevitable nuts. Nuts were warming, according to my mother, grandmother and all the ladies of the house, and winter was the best time to eat them. They were freshest then too, having been harvested in the autumn.

These were not nuts you could grab by the fistful and shove into your mouth. No, you had to work for each and every one of them as they came in their shells. The shells could be tossed into the fire-place, which was fun, but the peeling was sometimes harder. *Chilghozas* (pine nuts) demanded the most time and concentration and I liked them the best, especially the raw, untoasted ones with their soft white flesh and green inner core. My preference then ran to walnuts, especially the *kaghzi akhrote* or 'paper-shell' variety. These could be crushed between two hands without help from a nutcracker. As I picked out the flesh from the mess of crushed shell, my mother would remind me, 'Always eat walnuts with raisins or you will get . . .' 'I know, I know,' I would answer, 'a sore throat.' There would be peanuts too, freshly roasted in *karhais* (woks) filled with sand, and pistachios from Iran, the best in the world.

The nuts were not always enough, so a servant would be dispatched to the distant kitchen for plates of *pakoris,* vegetable fritters made by dipping vegetables or slices of them in a spicy chickpea flour batter and deep-frying them. We would shout in the general direction of the servant's departing back, 'Ask the cook to make extra green chilli *pakoris.*' The *pakoris* were eaten by most with fresh green mint chutney but for those of us who wanted to set our mouths ablaze, a bite into a hot chilli *pakori* after a bite of a sliced potato *pakori* was the perfect pairing.

Soon all the guests who did not live at Number 7 would begin to depart. My grandfather would take his last sip of whisky and say to no-one in particular, 'Have the food put on the table.' After a while the servant who had taken the order would return, salaam my grandfather and announce, '*Sa'ab*, the food is on the table.' We would all get up and start ambling towards the dining room annexe in small groups.

In the dining room was a long, formal dining table. Joined to it were two other dining tables of decreasing quality. There was a chair for my grandfather at the head of the formal table, a chair for my grandmother to his left and more chairs for the grown-ups on either side. Further down, at the tables of lesser quality generally reserved for the children, chairs gave way to benches. We children were so far away from the head of the table that I did not know until I was told years later that my grandmother was a vegetarian and had invented the East-West dish, spicy cauliflower gratinéed with cheese, that we all loved so much. We could hardly hear or see what was going on at my grandfather's end. We made note of Babaji's bobbing white beard but we were too busy with our own discussions to pay the upper end of the table much heed. I did know one thing though. My grandfather didn't drink water with his meals. He drank Club Soda. We saw it being poured.

Whatever was cooked in the kitchen's large *pateelas* (pots) came to the dining room in recurring serving dishes, two or three to each of the tables. There was hardly a question of courses. Everything savoury was part of the main course and came to the tables at the same time. Fresh fruit and sometimes carrot *halwa* in the winter followed.

Winter dinners often included game, as the men were avid hunters. There might be duck, partridge or quail, some with pellets still inside them, cooked with rich, cardamom-flavoured sauces. My father's favourite was leg of wild boar, cooked for a whole day in beer, but most of the time it was the usual goat and potato curry, a standard and much loved staple. Accompanying it might be cauliflower with peas, carrots with fenugreek greens and some spinach, all to be eaten with *phulkas*, little puffed whole-wheat breads. We rarely had rice at night.

Special needs were catered for as well, such as soup for a sick child. Once, when Taiji was on a diet to control her ballooning weight, her meat was boiled, and instead of eating it with Indian bread, she wrapped each morsel in lettuce leaves.

I began to notice a disturbing pattern. Very often, choice pieces of meat were missing. Marrow bones, pieces of fish-shaped muscle (the best meat), where were they? I would look around in the serving dish and find nothing I wanted. Then I would see Taiji come in from the kitchen with a small bowl and quietly spoon out these very pieces to just her own three children, Raghudada, Sheila and Rajesh. Indignant and unable to deal with what I perceived as unfairness, I would look up at my mother but she would blink her eyes, suggesting I be quiet.

At night, as I undressed for bed, I would complain bitterly to Bauwa but she would hush me up – Taiji's room was just next door – and say something like, 'You had enough to eat, didn't you?' or 'Once we get back to Kanpur you can have whatever you want.'

If Taiji was trying to compensate her children with choice foods for their emotional deprivations, this could be written off as one of the smaller ripples created by Shibbudada's behaviour towards his family. As we all got older, the ripples would reach further and further and enmesh Shibbudada's family and ours in the worst tangle of human relationships.

CHAPTER THIRTEEN

Family Picnics in Delhi ✻ *The Art of Getting Thirty People into Two Cars* ✻ *Cinema Trips* ✻ *Story Time*

We all looked forward to family picnics in Delhi. They helped to cloud nagging worries, to take minds off the daily grind.

The best time for picnics was during the winter when the days were sunny and crisp, but the monsoon season, with its romantic, cool, moisture-laden breezes, was just as attractive. Our chosen destination was rarely some glorious wilderness. No, when we were in Delhi, we preferred familiar territory, perhaps the well-tended garden of an eighteenth-century tomb or a twelfth-century palace on the outskirts of our own beloved city, which affirmed our deep connection to the land and its history, to our sense of entitlement. The entire family went on these picnics. During my childhood it didn't occur to me that families came in sizes smaller than thirty people, swelling beatifically to a few thousand at the mere hint of a grand event.

Preparations for the picnic would begin at dawn. All the short ladies of the house – and they were all short – would begin scurrying around in the kitchen. One would be stirring potatoes in a gingery tomato sauce; another sitting on a low stool, rolling out *pooris* (small puffed breads for deep-frying) by the dozen; yet another would be forming meatballs with wetted palms. Pickles had to be removed from pickling jars, fruit packed in baskets and disposable terracotta *mutkainas* (handle-less cups for our water and tea) given a thorough rinse.

I would run from the kitchen, where the smells promised future pleasures, to where the servants were packing the charcoal and *ungeethis* (braziers). From here I would make a dash for the garage where the boots of the cars were being coaxed to hold the *durees* (cotton rugs), sheets, pots, pans – indeed a whole *batterie de cuisine pique-nique*. The servants were all masters at it by now, and carried on with military precision.

Two cars, the gleaming Dodge and the Ford, would stand at the ready in the brick driveway with Masoom Ali, Babaji's fez-hatted driver, giving last-minute flicks with a duster to the cars' exteriors.

The art of getting thirty people into two cars had long been mastered. The first layer consisted of alternating short ladies and teenage children, with the teenagers sitting perched on the edge of the seat. On the laps of the ladies and teenagers went the slim ten- to twelve-year-olds. The third layer, sitting on the laps of the second layer, consisted of those under ten. The tall men and servants sat in the front seat. On their laps sat the fat ten- to twelve-year-olds holding all the baskets and pots that could not be stuffed into the boot.

The cars would grunt and groan but always start. The Ford would lead the Dodge through the northern Kashmiri Gate of the Old City, past St James's Church built by a nineteenth-century Anglo-Indian, past Shah Jahan's seventeenth-century Red Fort and out of the Old City through its southern Delhi Gate. Soon we would be travelling along the wide, tree-lined boulevards of Lutyens's New Delhi. It was from here that British governor-generals and viceroys, known by the Indians as *Laat Sa'abs* (Lord Sahibs), ruled from their own, Lutyens-designed, pink sandstone palace in a setting one

Englishman described as 'the court of the Great Moghul run with the quiet precision of the court of St James'. Beneath the entire four-and-a-half acre palatial building (the palace is now the official residence of the Indian president) ran a full Edwardian basement – a downstairs to the upstairs – replete with domestic offices, sculleries, bakeries, larders, even a press to spew out streams of menus. Bands played when these viceroys came down to dinner, with one particular ruler choosing *The Roast Beef of Old England*. (We children *did* get something out of all this. Whenever someone was acting too grand we would put them down with, 'Don't be such a *Laat Sa'ab*'.)

Our cars would now head towards open fields of mustard and millet (these have given way to concrete as the city's population has grown from less than a million to over twelve million). Well before we got there, far away in the distance and standing upright like a welcoming beacon, could be seen the tower towards which we were heading. This was the Qutb Minar, built in the twelfth century by the first Muslim dynasty to rule Hindu India.

The cars would pull up beside the gardens and unload their passengers. The short ladies, coming out last, would inhale the fresh country air and, with their hands, try vainly to iron out their now very crushed sarees. While the children rushed to climb the tall sandstone tower, the short ladies would amble to the base of the tower, touch it to establish that they had been there and, having exerted themselves enough, stroll back to the garden to pick a site for the picnic. A large, cotton, blue and red-striped *duree* would be spread out and on it laid a slightly smaller white sheet.

From the top of the tower we children could proprietorially survey all the Delhis below us. This was our city. There was the thirteenth-century Delhi of the Khilji dynasty, the fourteenth-century fort of the Tughlak dynasty, the fifteenth-century tombs of the Lodhi dynasty, the sixteenth-century tomb of the Moghul emperor Humayun, Shah Jahan's seventeenth-century mosque and then British India with its elegant avenues and circular shopping centre, Connaught Place.

Soon our eyes, impelled by our stomachs, would settle on something closer – a brightly edged cotton *duree* over which hovered some familiar short ladies. We would think of the meatballs cooked with cumin, coriander and yoghurt and come thundering down the hundreds of steps.

As we settled down cross-legged on the edges of the *duree*, the servants would lay out the freshly heated food. We rarely used plates or cutlery for eating. Instead, we would take two *pooris* at a time, using the first as a plate, a kind of mediaeval trencher, and the second to make our little morsels.

Meanwhile Jai Singh would be making tea in a kettle set on top of an *ungeethi* (brazier). After our meal, we would hold out our terracotta *mutkainas* towards him, making sure to wrap them in our handkerchiefs first so our fingers would not burn, and Jai Singh would pour . . . steamy hot tea, milky and sweet, so hot that we would have to start by breathing in tiny little sips.

Indian movies encouraged another kind of picnic, a mini-picnic of a more informal, impromptu nature. When we were in Delhi, we never saw movies with our parents, only with our cousins. An older cousin acted as escort and was given the task of buying tickets, generally for the upstairs balcony.

Movies were just an extension of story-telling, which was

second nature to most of us in the quill-and-ink set. We didn't grow up with bedtime stories. That sort of cosy intimacy was hardly possible with twenty or so bedded-down children. Our experience of story-telling was more of a family huddle in the middle of the day. We would drag an aunt or uncle to a sofa and drape ourselves around them – on the arms and back of the sofa, on the carpet below, on their laps – a little hillock of overlapping bodies, hanging on every word. 'Please, please, tell us another story.' Their fund of riddles, poems and anecdotes seemed endless.

My aunt Saran Bhua's husband was an accomplished golfer who impressed us no end with his plus fours and beret. He would hardly be home from a round of golf when we would corner him to regale us with folksy tales told in the *purabia* dialect of his home state, Uttar Pradesh. One of his stories that we loved to hear again and again had to do with his trip to England with an Indian athletic team. At a grand dinner, all heads of foreign delegations were asked to sing their national anthems in 'their native languages'. 'What could I sing?' he would say. 'Our national anthem then was *God Save the King* and it was in English. So I sang this . . .' And he would proceed with his rendition of a folk song he had taught us all so we could join in, '*Bibi maindaki ri, tu tow pani may ki rani*' ('O Lady Frog, You are the Queen of the Waters').

My cousin Mahesh's paternal grandmother looked most dignified and formidable with her shock of white hair, her straight back, her peg leg and her cane, but her whispered tales rocked us with giggles as they were full of the naughtiest, scatological humour. Shibbudada's yarns were either about musicians or the training of musicians: 'So-and-so could not look his guru in the eye; he was not allowed to play a single note for ten years,' or about hiking across the Himalayas, another of his passions.

We children made up our own stories too. Sometimes they took the form of plays, which we enacted for our enthusiastic elders, setting up curtains, arranging seating and even selling tickets. No mean reviews here! Our very first play, when our proportions must have been diminutive, used the space between the four legs of a roll-top desk in Shibbudada's annexe as a stage! This was still in the days of innocence, well before I had learnt to question my contradictory uncle.

Film-going was just another step. We liked all movies but going to Hindi movies had added benefits. These Indian films were particularly conducive to whetting and then satisfying our appetites. They generally lasted about four hours. Whole families, including infants, would come to view the mythological-historical-tragi-comical musicals. There was a great deal of yelling, crying, getting up, singing along and sitting down in the audience throughout the show. Certainly no-one minded the noisy unwrapping of paper cones containing *chane jor garam*, small chickpeas that had been flattened and roasted, then flavoured with cumin, chilli powder, sour mango powder and black rock salt. We would munch on the chickpeas as we watched Hanuman, the Monkey God, fly across a dark sky dotted equidistantly with hundreds of five-pointed stars, all cut from the same stencil.

During the long intermission we would all go in a horde to buy potato patties, *aloo-ki-tikiyas*, from vendors who had carefully posted themselves just outside the cinema doors. These patties were a Delhi speciality and their unique flavour depended partly on the way they were cooked and partly on the spices in the stuffing. They were not deep-fried or shallow-fried but pan-roasted instead.

Each vendor carried a brazier on which he had set up a large cast-iron griddle (*tava*). Patties that were ready to sell sat waiting on the outer fringes, staying warm until needed. Those that were still cooking were in the centre, sizzling away in a few tablespoons of oil that pooled in the middle. In one pot were the vendor's seasoned mashed potatoes, and in another the stuffing made out of highly spiced split peas that had been cooked until dry and crumbly. To make a patty, the vendor would pinch off a ball of mashed potatoes, flatten it into a small patty, pinch off a smaller ball of the stuffing and place it in the centre. Then he would cover up the stuffing with the potato and make a ball. The ball was then flattened and slapped onto the griddle.

The squatting vendor kept turning each patty this way and that until it was reddish brown and completely crisp on both sides. By this time our mouths could almost taste the *tikiyas*. As soon as he got the order, the vendor would place a patty on a leaf, split it open and smother both parts with sweet and sour tamarind chutney. We would carry these hot patties back into the dark cinema house and eat them as we watched Hanuman trying to rescue Sita, the good queen, from the clutches of the demon King of Sri Lanka.

CHAPTER FOURTEEN

Summer Holidays in the Hills ❁ The Great Exodus
Grandmother's Magic Potion ❁ Mountain Picnics
The Taste of Ecstasy

During the same eight years that we shuttled between our homes in Delhi and Kanpur, we spent our summer holidays – three or more glorious months of them – in 'the hills'. The official version of this custom had started in 1864 when the British government, unable to suffer the heat of 'the plains', moved the entire administration up to Simla in the central Himalayas for the 'summer', a good six months that went from April to early October. Seventeenth-century Moghul emperors, also originally outsiders from colder climes, had set a precedent. In a mighty cavalcade of elephants, horses and camels, these rulers had travelled annually even further north, to Srinagar – a lake-filled valley in the heart of Kashmir. Once there, they had quickly declared, 'If there be a Paradise on earth/It is this, it is this, it is this.' For the British, who governed India first from Calcutta and then from New Delhi, a similar cooling respite was provided by the hill town of Simla.

Known as Shimla today and in the state of Himachal Pradesh, the area once contained a few small hamlets and, on top of the highest peak, Jakko, a temple dedicated to the goddess Kali. Though sparsely populated by humans, nature was fully represented in its resplendent glory, providing stately forests of deodars, pines and oaks and a profusion of rhododendrons that climbed all the way up to the snowline.

The early nineteenth century was to see a war here between local chiefs and the Nepalese Gurkhas, and then, when the British came to the aid of the chiefs, between the Gurkhas and the British. Leading the British to their final victory was Major General Sir David Ochterlony, the same gentleman who would insist on hiring my grandfather's grandfather in Delhi somewhat later. The first cottage was built in Simla in 1819 by an assistant political agent for hill states, Lt Ross. As more and more English officials visited, an increasing number of British-style cottages with very British gardens sprang up to accommodate them. The main road was called the Mall and the town developed the feel of a British transplant.

Around April and May, when scorching *loo* winds swirled hellishly in the plains, Britons began leaving in droves and heading north. Army battalions were stationed in the hills for the summer so they could rest and recuperate. British businessmen tried their best to flee the plains but if they could not, they sent their wives and children. In the government, everyone from the viceroy down to the petty officers packed their bags and travelled to the Himalayas. The viceroy had a domed sandstone palace in Delhi to stand up to the grand remnants of Moghul architecture. In Simla, he took refuge in a more English mansion with a countrified name to match its appearance: Viceregal Lodge. As the High Court moved up too, my grandfather, as eminent barrister, followed. His business was now in the hills. Besides, it was cool and much more pleasant.

As Babaji was the head of the family, if he moved, we all moved. Oddly enough, he never built a house in Simla or in any other hill station. He rented instead, not one large house but two or three adjacent ones according to the number of people expected that year. These houses – nestling in the mountains and surrounded by sun-kissed dahlias and hydrangeas, with semi-British names like 'Choor View' and 'Pentland' – came with only basic furniture. This meant that everything else, including the servants, had to come from Delhi. The contents of kitchens, bedrooms and bathrooms, along with toys and games, were all put in trunks, canvas holdalls, baskets and bundles. The whole army of forty or so people, all in a state of excitement as we loved the hills, would then embark on the annual exodus. We would take the overnight train to Kalka, in the foothills of the Himalayas. At 2400 feet above sea level, it already hinted at the pleasures to come. There we would have a British Railways breakfast in the waiting rooms – generally slightly greasy eggs, toast and tea served on heavy railway crockery – and then pile into the eight or nine cars that had been hired for the four-hour drive.

The first sight of the Himalayan peaks towering over the plains, range after purple range, was exhilarating enough. But as the procession of cars started up those hairpin bends, as the air got cooler, as we saw the first pines, the first ferns, the first waterfalls and gushing mountain streams, as we climbed to six, seven, then eight thousand feet above sea level, as the first mist licked our cars, each one of us, separately and together, felt that this was our paradise.

Some of us with delicate constitutions got a little nauseous on those hairpin bends. But there was no need to worry; my grand-mother had a cure. She would call a halt to the moving procession. 'Jai Singh, Jai Singh, where is the lime pickle?' she would yell out. Everyone would start jumping out of their cars. A break felt good.

Jai Singh, who knew where every last spoon was located, would quickly get his hands on the to-be-opened-on-the-journey basket. There, in a crock, would be Bari Bauwa's homemade lime pickle.

I (second from left) stand next to Veena embraced by Kailashdada's
wife, Manno Bhabi, and Sheila, at one of our Himalayan rented residences,
with glazed verandah in the background.

Black with age and with black pepper, cloves and cardamom, it was my grandmother's magic potion. She administered tiny portions of it and nausea just vanished. She had many such tricks up her sleeve. I was once bitten by a bee. I yelled with pain and my grandmother came running. The next thing I knew she was stroking my afflicted cheek and reciting some Sanskrit verse. I couldn't understand a word but it cured me quickly. She was a useful short lady to have around.

As new houses were rented each time, the first thrills were provided by the exploration of their nearly always damp and musty, unaired interiors. How many bathrooms? What sort of toilets? Enough tables to play bridge and rummy? Oh well, the floor would do. Was there a glazed verandah? We could not live without a glazed verandah.

Glazed verandahs were verandahs enclosed with glass windows to protect them, when necessary, from the cold and monsoon downpours. When the sun shone, all the windows could be flung open. Most hill houses had them, either running along one side of the house or, if we were lucky, along all four sides. We children lived in the verandahs and sometimes slept in them too. They gained such a grip on my psyche that when my husband and I bought our country house in upstate New York, the first room I added to take advantage of southern and western exposures was a hill station-style glazed verandah!

Once everyone had settled in and unpacked, the children were pretty much left to themselves, to explore mountain pathways, hike, cycle, ride and walk. No cars were allowed beyond a base point on most hill stations, including Simla, so we all had to move our own bodies around. It was considered healthy and, along with the fresh air, the main reason for our presence.

My boy cousins and I might decide to go to the Wood Bazaar (*Lakkar Bazaar*) and order new yo-yos. Here we would marvel as the carpenter, using just a lathe, transformed a block of wood right in front of our eyes into any sized yo-yo we requested. He would then lacquer it in the colours that suited us that day. I could never twirl and unfurl the yo-yos like my boy cousins or make them 'walk' or 'talk' or whatever else the boys did, but I could hold them in my hands and admire their shiny, smooth oranges, pinks and blues. We could take a walk past Scandal Point and the Ridge, past the Gaiety Theatre (where many years later I was to film the theatre scene in the Merchant Ivory movie, *Shakespeare Wallah*), go to the tallest peak in the region, Jakko Top, and stare at the hundreds of monkeys that gathered there around the Temple of Hanuman to stare right back at us.

Boys sport shorts and girls solar topees *on a mountain picnic.*
Typical picnic fare would be curry patties and poo*ris, the latter used as plates.*

The only organized activity in the hills was the mountain picnic, which was quite different from the city picnic.

The picnic site was carefully chosen weeks in advance, usually by Shibbudada who was well-versed in the terrain and remained our major-domo in the hills. Sometimes it was a distant mountain peak, several ranges away; at other times a thunderous waterfall in a deep valley; once it was a mountain stream rushing through a remote gorge. Ordinary picnic spots, where most mortals went, were never considered good enough. No, not in the hills. Our spots were picked not only for their natural grandeur but also for their inaccessibility in terms of distance or the climbing required.

Preparations for the picnic would also begin weeks in advance. Rickshaws and hill-palanquins (*daandees*) were arranged for the old and the infirm, and horses for the riders. The ladies of the house,

Family picnics in the 'hills' of the Himalayas often involved long hikes.
Here the walkers among us pose with Shibbudada (in the hat).
I am in the front row, far left, resting on a very handy stick.

plus numerous servants, spent many days preparing the food. Baskets of mangoes were ordered from various North Indian cities: *langras* from Benares for those who liked their mangoes tart; *dussehris* from Lucknow for those who liked them sweet and smooth; and *chusnis*, small sucking mangoes for those who preferred not to eat the fruit at all but to suck the juice straight from the skin. Lychees were ordered from the city that grew the juiciest, smallest-stoned varieties, Dehradun.

At sunrise, when the mountains were still shrouded in an icy mist, porters (*qoolies*), rickshaws, palanquins and horses were all assembled. First the porters were loaded with baskets of food and sent off with a party of servants. The walkers, led by Shibbudada who had a passion for hiking, would leave next. I chose to go with

Paddling in a stream on a picnic with Rajesh.
I have embroidered my shirt with a very stylish anchor.

him but nearly always lagged behind which made him very cross. Third were those who rode in the rickshaws and palanquins, and the last group consisted of those on horseback.

Clad in heavy sweaters, mufflers and shawls, our large party moved slowly, making numerous stops along the way. If we passed an orchard, a stop would be called and the farmer asked if we might pick plums or apricots for a certain sum. My favourite groves were those of almond trees. I loved green almonds, slit open and robbed of their tender, white flesh.

We would generally arrive at our picnic spot around midday. If it was beside a waterfall or stream, the children were allowed to swim while lunch was unpacked. The mangoes were placed in nooks of the stream to cool and fires were lit to heat certain dishes (and also to warm the children when they emerged from the freezing water). Then the meal, often including ground goat meat cooked with peas (*keema mattar*) and cauliflower cooked with fresh ginger, would be served, frequently accompanied by tales of adventure and hilarious stories about our ancestors.

The best part of the meal was still to come: those mangoes biding their time in the frigid waters. At the start of the season we had the choicest *dussehris* and *langras*, standard bearers of the northern mango world, peeled and cut into slices by the women. By the season's end all that was left on the market were the small, visually unprepossessing *chusnis*, the sucking mangoes. After lunch we would rush to the stream to peer at our final course, dozens of mottled, yellow-green, egg-shaped wonders, nestling on the pebbles just beneath the surface of the rippling, gurgling waters. We would each pick one out and roll it between our palms to soften the flesh and reduce it to juice. Then we would pluck off the very top, where the mango was once attached to a tree, put that top to our mouths and squeeze. Cool and sweet, this nectar had the taste of ecstasy, the ecstasy of our summers in the hills.

CHAPTER FIFTEEN

A New School ✳ Classmates in Burquas
Hindi or Urdu: a Dreadful Choice ✳ A Lethally Sharp Pencil

Leaving Kanpur in 1944 had been hard, as we knew it was for keeps. None of us ever went back there except in our dreams. For months afterwards, I would wake up in our new, much smaller home at Number 5, crying. My mother would move from her bed to mine and say, 'Were you dreaming of being in Kanpur again?' I would sob even louder. I felt I would never recover from the loss.

My life in our gardens, my shimmering Diwali oil lamps, my salmon-coloured dining room, my intimate world – it had all come to an end. Verging on my teens, I had to face a bustling cosmopolitan city without my older sisters who had been such calming companions. I did have my brothers now but they were already in college, dealing with their own lives and loves. My baby sister Veena was too young for pre-teen conversation.

School, yet again, was a problem. My father first put me in what he thought might be a continuation of the tried-and-tested convent school, the Convent of Jesus and Mary in New Delhi.

I lasted a month. The school was cruelly segregated then. Education was carried out in two unequal 'sections', the English and the Indian. My father must have got a guarantee that I would be put in the English section, which had the better teachers and students, though the thought of my father wanting me to be there was demeaning enough for me. After just a few days in this English section, which comprised mostly English girls but a few Indian daughters of high government officials as well, the school decided to transfer me to the Indian section. There were only Indians here under an Anglo-Indian teacher named Mrs Clock. I was even more confused and angry. No-one in this section could read, write or add. Where was I?

I complained daily to my father. In the end, he pulled me out and enrolled me in Queen Mary's Higher Secondary School. Although not a convent, it was still a missionary school, run this time by lay Episcopalians for the rather unique purpose of educating 'purdah girls', inner-city Muslim girls who wore the veil.

How such girls were educated at all was a wonder. Our Hindu family had, out of necessity, adopted many Muslim codes. Purdah, in its mildest version, had played its part. According to stories told by my two youngest aunts – my father's sisters, Saran Bhua and Kiran Bhua – their father, my grandfather, had decided to send them to college, the same one he had attended, St Stephen's College. Not so easy. First, the girls had to get out of their house in the Old City with its very Muslim sensibilities. My grandfather's grand phaeton was summoned to the nearest road that could accommodate it and servants held up sheets on both sides of my aunts, to shield them from the gaze of men, as they manoeuvred the narrower lanes. Once in college, where they were the only two female students, two chairs were placed for them as near the professor as possible. They could play tennis if they wished but only with each other and after the courts had been cleared of male students for the duration of their match.

By the time I went to Queen Mary's, Hindu girls certainly had much more freedom, but for Muslim inner-city girls, even getting to a good school was full of hazards. Queen Mary's solved the problem by sending a small, horse-driven, curtained van to collect them. I remember that rickety van as it clattered back into the school grounds. A door at the rear would be impatiently shoved open from the inside and a dozen or more girls – shadowy, unrecognizable forms swathed in white, dark green or black *burkas* (body-covering chadors) – would burst out, hopping down one after the other. Once inside the school doors, they would race down the hall, tearing off the constricting *burkas* as they ran. There was a special corridor leading to the back netball court where hooks had been strategically placed on both sides. This is where the *burkas* were hung – long, haphazard rows of shrouds.

Queen Mary's meant that in my schooling, I was moving from a Western, Christian world to a more Indian, Christian one. The school was Christian in name and intent for sure. But because only the heads of the school were Christian, and Indian independence was already on the cards, Indians were increasingly allowed to be themselves – Hindu, Muslim, Sikh or whatever.

My first, seemingly insurmountable, hurdle at school was something else entirely. In the Middle School, all subjects – history, geography, mathematics, everything except English – were taught in either Hindi or Urdu, Indian languages I had spoken at home since I uttered my first words but had never learnt to write or read.

First I had to choose between Hindi and Urdu. Hindi was part of my Hindu inheritance, the language that had evolved from classical Sanskrit. Urdu was part of our Muslim culture, a hybrid that had developed in the bazaars of Moghul Delhi, my very own city. It used the grammar of Hindi but borrowed much of its vocabulary from Persian and Arabic. One was the language of my mother and the women of our house; the other, because of Delhi's peculiar history, the language of my father and most of my male relatives. Partly inspired by Shibbudada's passion for Urdu poetry, I had studied the Urdu alphabet once. A *maulvi* (Muslim teacher) would come to Number 7, make me whitewash a wooden board and then, with a freshly sharpened *qalam* (quill) dipped in an ink I made myself by dissolving ink tablets in water, teach me to write my alphabet: *alif, bay, pay, they, tay*. I had got as far as being able to read and write simple words.

It was a dreadful choice for me. I loved the elegant sounds of Urdu but, employing perhaps the only gene for farsightedness I possessed, I opted for Hindi. Until then, to be among the brightest in my class had seemed almost a birthright. Yet here I was at twelve, at the bottom of the class, struggling with a new alphabet. I was in the uniquely embarrassing position of not being able to read or write in school.

My father hired a Hindi master who came every other day on a bicycle. As our lives at Number 5 and Number 7 were hopelessly intertwined, it was decided that the best place for me to study quietly would be in one of the unused rooms in Number 7's south annexe. Shibbudada's suite was at the river end, and the room where I studied was at the opposite end. A table and chair had been set up there for the purpose.

I started with the Hindi alphabet, a, aa, e, ee, o, oo. I struggled. My masterji (the 'ji' was added as a mark of respect) struggled. I was learning, but very slowly. Every now and then my youngest sister, Veena, who was about seven by now and in the same school as I was, would get on her bicycle at Number 5, cross the road, come down the long driveway lined with henna hedges and wave at me through the door as I studied with masterji. Masterji took to inviting her in, playing with her and teasing her.

The corner room of the annexe at Number 7 where I studied Hindi.
The annexe also housed extra bedrooms, the library (with the family history)
and Shibbudada's suite. The garden is decorated with lights for a wedding.

One day she came in and idly picked up my pencil as she and masterji bantered. Masterji lifted her up and was teasing her when somehow – no-one knew quite how it happened – the point of my pencil was in his eyeball. I have always liked to keep my pencils lethally sharpened. He screamed in pain, Veena began to cry and I felt miserable because it was my pencil and my sister. He pulled the pencil out and dabbed his eye. I offered to call a doctor but he insisted on going home right away. He did not return for several weeks. When he did, his eye seemed healed but he remained so cross about the incident that he could barely teach. Soon he stopped coming altogether. That was the end of my Hindi lessons.

I was left too agitated to start again with another teacher. I told my father I would manage. After all, anyone who knows the Hindi alphabet can read it. It is a completely phonetic, logical language.

Of course, my writing was pitiful, I read very slowly and my knowledge of the more 'Sanskritized' vocabulary that pure Hindi demanded was still nil. But I soldiered on. Within a year I could just about keep up with my classmates.

CHAPTER SIXTEEN

Shibbudada's Favourites ❋ Teatime Tension ❋ A Dream House in Daurala ❋ The Sugar Cane Welds ❋ Sweets Galore in the Sugar Factory

Shibbudada continued to haunt my life with a presence I both wanted and didn't want. The seeds of the slow-developing rift between our families were also being sown.

It was not enough for Shibbudada just to ignore his wife and children. Every now and then he needed the warmth of a family, and he picked ours. We were all, on the whole, good-looking, well-mannered, neat and clean. He liked that. I remember him saying once to a roomful of listeners, hanging on his words, 'He has such a thick, coarse neck. How could he possibly appreciate the finer things of life – poetry, music?' He made statements like that. Most people just laughed and went along.

All members of my father's family had thin, delicate necks. That must have been a plus. In my father he had an adoring younger brother who never learnt to deny him anything he asked for. My mother was sweet, pretty and pliant. We were his ready-made family when he needed us.

Shibbudada went further. Out of my parent's six children, he picked two to bless with his special glow, thereby driving small wedges between us that would grow into greater resentments.

Of the two brothers my parents had left in his care, his

Kamal (left) and Lalit, leaning on the falsa tree
in the garden of Number 5.

favour was bestowed on the younger, Bhaiyyadada. My eldest
brother, Brijdada, always a bit of an introvert, was quiet and
thoughtful. He liked to paint and draw, which were not Shibbudada's
interests. Bhaiyyadada was a total extrovert, full of jokes and fun,
easy-going and utterly charming.

Among the girls, his eye fell on Kamal. Lalit was startlingly
beautiful too with wavy hair and dark eyes that glowed with intelligence. He liked her. But it was Kamal who had an unearthly, angelic
innocence and a face to match. I remember that, even at the age of
seventeen, she thought babies came directly out of the stomach.
Perhaps the convent's nuns could be credited with this bit of
fantasy. She had shy, undemanding eyes, a fine aquiline nose, thin,
well-shaped lips and a firm chin. As her body began to fill out, it too

My brother Bhaiyyadada.

followed a divine master plan. Rather like the goddesses that cling to temple brackets, she managed a large bust, tiny waist and rounded hips. She had it all. And, in our joint family setup, she was Shibbudada's favourite.

Bhaiyyadada and Kamal could walk into Shibbudada's annexe freely. He could be seen laughing with them, with his arms on their shoulders. They had an ease between them that few others shared. What his children and wife were thinking all this time can only be imagined.

Shibbudada had, some time back, given up his law practice. As he himself explained, his delicate constitution was incapable of pleading the causes of thick-necked crooks forever. He had, instead, started a finance and leasing company. At first, the business was situated near Kashmiri Gate and then, as it grew wildly successful, the family bought a building in Lutyens-designed Connaught Place in New Delhi and the business moved there.

On his way back from the office in the early evening, Shibbudada had taken to stopping off at Number 5 where my mother would ask him politely if he'd like some tea, even though we might have had ours earlier. Our smaller meals were in Number 5 now but we still went to Number 7 for lunch and dinner. After his tea with us, Shibbudada would drive on to his annexe in Number 7 to rest, change and then go out for the evening. His wife, Taiji, hardly ever saw him.

Once Taiji discovered that Shibbudada was making a habit of stopping off at Number 5 for tea, she started keeping a lookout for him from Number 7's front verandah. If she managed to spot his familiar cream and blue Chevy turning into our much smaller, bricked driveway, she would begin walking slowly towards our house, a casual look on her face as if she had just thought of coming over to greet our family. The weight of her large body would shift in heaves from one side to the other as she moved.

As Shibbudada settled down in our drawing room, I would look nervously through a window and see what I knew I would see: Taiji advancing along Number 7's red gravel driveway. My stomach would knot up in a state of the highest anxiety. I could barely get the tea down my throat.

When Taiji arrived, all bathed and freshened up for the evening, Shibbudada, as expected, would not greet her or look at her. He proceeded as if she was not there. My mother would sweetly pour some tea for her as well while trying to ignore the prevailing tension. After tea, Shibbudada joked with us, asked us about school, told funny stories, and offered all manner of wonderful fruit – mangoes, cherries, lychees or loquats or whatever he had brought especially for us from the most expensive fruit shop in Delhi, Oriental Stores. I would be at a loss to know which emotion to project, the I-am-so-happy-to-receive-the-gifts look to Shibbudada or the I-don't-want-them-take-them-for-your-children look to Taiji. My palms would begin to sweat. What I felt was acute misery.

After tea, Shibbudada would say a merry goodbye to us, get into his car and drive off to Number 7, leaving Taiji to walk back slowly on her own.

M y father had taken on the job of general manager at one of North India's largest sugar factories in Daurala, just outside the city of Meerut, and so avoided this recurring scene in the family drama. For most of the time he was not there at all. My mother stayed with us because of school but we joined our father whenever we could.

In Daurala, far from his powerful relatives, my father shut out that world and once again created one of his dream homes. The house was a sprawling but very basic brick structure, entirely surrounded for miles by sugar cane fields. Way in the distance could be seen the outlines of a dense guava grove. Other than that, there was nothing but the blue of the sky, the chirping of birds and the sounds of pumps gushing water out of the earth. The sugar factory was such a distance away that we could neither see it nor hear it.

My father built a large chicken coop in the back courtyard with plenty of baby chicks to greet us whenever we visited. In the walled vegetable garden, he had the gardener put in strawberries, which seemed most exotic and desirable to us. We only visited Daurala during our shorter holidays. My father missed my mother. He didn't even know how to fall ill without her. If his temperature reached anywhere near a hundred, he would start moaning, 'Hai, hai.' My mother's gentle ministrations were needed to calm him down. She tried to spend as much time with him as possible. Whenever she went, she took my sister Veena and me along. If it was holiday time, Lalit, Kamal, Brijdada and Bhaiyyadada came too.

Once ensconced in the house, our favourite destinations were the sugar cane fields and, if we wanted a longer walk, the guava orchard. The sugar cane was so tall we'd get lost between the rows of stalks. The thin, long leaves scratched our arms. A field-hand would cut us a cane; we would peel it with our teeth and proceed to crush the juice out as we chewed on one end. We could then wash our sticky hands at a water pump and perhaps wet our feet as well. Our brothers, if they were there, brought their guns along and shot at the little black *tiliyar* (rather like ortolans), which we all considered a rare delicacy.

Sugar cane was a winter crop as were the guavas. We grew some of the best guavas – large, round, pale-green balls that my sisters and I liked to bite into when they were still jaw-breakingly hard. The softer, fully ripe ones we took home to my mother who instantly made *chaat* out of them. It was easy enough to do. We would stand around, eyes glued to her hands, mouths watering in anticipation, as she peeled the guavas, the skin coming off in long snakes, and then cut them into dice. She put these into a bowl, adding salt, pepper, ground roasted cumin seeds, chilli powder, lime juice and just a tiny bit of sugar. She mixed all this thoroughly with her hands, sometimes sprinkling in a few drops of water so the spices would adhere better. Then she would serve the guava *chaat* to us on a plate and stick toothpicks in as eating implements.

It was the toothpicks, used in the bazaars of Old Delhi in place of forks, that transformed homemade *chaat* into the illicit bazaar *chaat* which my father had, with his repeated, ominous warnings, forbidden us to eat as it 'carried diseases'. As we placed a piece of spicy guava in our mouths we could taste the toothpick and the illicit bazaar. My mother knew just how to add extra flavour to a simple treat.

Sometimes my brothers, armed with their double-barrelled guns and their twelve-bore cartridges, would hop onto the small sugar cane trains that ran through the fields and head out for distant lakes, looking for ducks, or go on deer and partridge shoots. At night, after we had feasted on some of the game, I would go to sleep with the sounds and smells of my brothers cleaning their guns and talking excitedly to my father about the hunt.

One day my father asked us if we would like to go to the sugar factory. Sugar and sugar cubes were made there by the ton. That would certainly be more interesting than watching the making of hydrogenated cooking fat, though I had to admit I did like seeing peanuts being pressed at my father's previous job. What Dadaji thought might draw our real interest this time was the tonnage of sweets that the factory also churned out. He had always brought some home and my mother had doled it out to us in small amounts.

At the factory, all such curbs vanished. Half the workers stopped what they were doing to greet the family, and each one pointed to hillocks of toffees, wrapped sweets, peppermints and lemon balls and said the same thing, 'Take, take. Take as much as you want.' We did. We kept eating sweets as we saw the sugar cane juice being boiled and thickened, as we witnessed white sugar cubes neatly packaged into boxes, as granulated sugar came pouring out of large metal tubes, as we went up and down the factory's metal steps. In the end we were so sick of sweets that hardly any of us eat it now. Sad to say that in the course of that single day, I lost my sweet tooth entirely, or almost entirely.

My father, too, had probably had his fill of fat and sugar as he eventually returned to Delhi and became the general manager of a cloth factory, Delhi Cloth Mills, also owned by family friends. From then on, instead of hydrogenated fat or bags of sugar, the household was never short of bolts of cloth acquired on the cheap.

CHAPTER SEVENTEEN

Visiting the Old City ※ The Lane of Fried Breads
Monsoon Mushrooms

Whenever my mother wanted to visit her own family home, she always said, 'Come *beta* [child], let's go to the city.' We knew what that meant: a visit to our *nana ka ghar* (maternal grandfather's house). Her father and mother had lived and died in the Old City, in a house where her eldest brother's family still resided. I think that, to her, the orchard site of her in-laws, beyond the city's walls and the northern Kashmiri Gate, would always be the suburbia of the la-de-da set into which she had, by good fortune, married.

It was usually just my mother, Veena and me on these city visits. The ritual generally began on a Saturday morning. After breakfast, my mother would remove the big silver key chain clipped to her waist and open her locked cupboard. Inside was a State Express 555 tin from which she would fill my father's silver cigarette case, tucking a row of cigarettes behind an elastic band. The cigarette case would be clicked shut and handed over to my father who hovered behind her. She would also remove some cash – whatever my father needed for the day – and place it in my father's palm. The cupboard would be relocked and the bunch of keys tucked back in the waist. My father would stride off to the car waiting to take him to his office.

My mother, ever elegant, in the back garden in Kanpur.

Freed of the household duties that she took very seriously, my mother would pull out her *attachee* case. (Yes, that is how we pronounced it. I thought it was an Indian word. I did not discover its French connection until I was fully grown.) Into this rectangular, leather box went a fresh cotton saree, my mother's knitting or sewing, a comb and a few gifts. Then my mother would disappear into her dressing room with its three-mirrored dressing table, and change into a printed silk saree.

I never understood this. Some odd sense of propriety had

convinced her that she should travel and arrive in silk, change into crisp cotton for the day and change back into flowing silk to return home.

By this time my father would have sent the car and driver back for us. My mother, smelling sweetly of Hazeline Vanishing Cream, would step into the car, *attachee* case in one hand, her handbag in the other.

My father almost never came with us or deigned to join us later in the evening. Although he had been raised in the Old City, it gave him no joy to return. A part of him viewed it as old-fashioned, germ-infested and dangerous.

The residential section of the Old City then, as now, was a maze of such narrow lanes that a cow and a human could barely pass each other. We would have to leave the car on a wider road at a fairly distant point with instructions to the driver about the time he could collect us at the end of the day. Then my mother and her two youngest children would walk. We would have to tread carefully, sidestepping sleeping dogs and oncoming cycle-rickshaws. If a shopkeeper decided to empty a bucketful of dirty water onto the lane, we expertly hopped out of the way as we simultaneously dodged a man carrying a hundred cardboard boxes on his head. If my mother stopped to buy sweets for her family, she knew enough to keep an eye on her handbag at all times. If we saw a street-sweeper approaching with her wild broom, we held handkerchiefs to our noses so we would not inhale the dust she raised. My mother walked at a steady pace, one hand gripping the *attachee* case, the other with the handbag, holding her saree a few inches off the questionable ground.

Our journey took us through the Lane of Fried Breads (*Parathe Vali Gulley*) where I always urged my mother to stop for a quick *paratha* (fried puffy bread) stuffed with fenugreek greens. There were two or three open-fronted shops, all with shallow *karhais* (woks) set up almost on the street, right where passers-by could be easily enticed. Inside the *karhais*, bobbing in a lake of hot *ghee* (clarified butter), were three or four big, fat, puffed-up *parathas*.

A word here about terminology. In our family, a small ball of whole-wheat dough deep-fried into a puffball was called a *poori*. If it was stuffed with spiced split peas, it was called a *bedvi*. A *paratha*, on the other hand, was a flat bread made on a *tava* or griddle, somewhat like a pancake. Why, on this lane alone, a *bedvi*, or stuffed *poori* if you will, was called a *paratha*, I do not know. And why, on this lane alone, was the *karhai* (wok), however shallow, called a *tava* (griddle)? Delhi was an ancient, idiosyncratic city. I never asked the questions and my mother never explained. My preoccupation then was that the *parathas*, or whatever anyone wished to call them, came stuffed with a choice of green peas, potatoes, fenugreek greens, chickpea flour, spiced split peas, cauliflower or grated white radish. Which one, or ones, would I choose? To make the choice even harder, combinations were also possible. All were expertly spiced; all were utterly delicious.

The peculiarity of these shops was that they charged only by the *paratha*. This had been the tradition since time immemorial, which in this case was 1875 when the first of these shops-cum-restaurants opened. The vegetables and condiments served with the *parathas* were free.

As my father frowned on all bazaar food, my mother would deny my request at first. But she herself was tempted by the smells and, if asked enough times, would capitulate with a certain relief. 'Just don't drink the water,' she would whisper, convincing herself that now she had dealt with my father's fears. We climbed up a few steps, went past a billboard reassuring us that only the purest 'real' *ghee* was used on the premises (as opposed to the kind my father had churned out in his factory) and took our seats at the rough wooden tables. A young man whizzed by, dropping *pattals* (plates made from semi-dried leaves) in front of us. He came by again, ladling out the chutneys and pickles with equal speed: sweet chutney made with dried green mango, dried pomegranate and dried jujubes; sour chutney made with fresh mint, green coriander and grated white radish; and carrot pickle made with carrots, yellow chillies, crushed mustard seeds and tamarind. Already on the table was some salt seasoned with ground roasted cumin and crushed red chillies.

Before any real food arrived, we would start dipping our fingers in the condiments and licking them. Then came the vegetables – meats did not belong in such places – carrots stir-fried with young fenugreek greens; potatoes and peas cooked with cumin, asafetida and tomatoes; cauliflower with ginger and green chillies. As soon as the vegetables were on our plates, the hot, hot *parathas* floated in, whichever we had ordered, all puffed up, ready to be deflated and devoured even before all the steam had hissed out.

My mother never allowed us to eat too much as we were, after all, on our way to spend the day with her family. This was just a taste to tide us over until lunchtime. But what a taste it was – vegetarian, pure Old Delhi and exclusively *Parathe Vali Gulley*.

We crisscrossed a few more narrow lanes before coming to the portals of our mother's family home, our *nana ka ghar*. There was no way anyone could gauge from the outside what the inside might have been like. The well-worn wooden double-doors were always shut. We would knock and a servant girl would come to unlatch them to let us in. As the doors closed again behind us, the pace of life slowed instantly and we seemed to enter an earlier world.

Our *nana ka ghar* was of the same basic design as other attached houses in the Old City. All the rooms, on several floors, were built around an inner courtyard that served to let in light and air. Wealthier homes had several intricately carved stone courtyards, one leading to the next, some even with gardens and trees in them. But my mother's home was modest. One courtyard – plain, undecorated and treeless – sufficed. The rooms were simple too, with Moghul-style arched niches for closets, and seating either on low divans covered with white sheets or on the floor with bolsters to lean against. The office room did have a desk but it was the short-legged kind that stayed on the floor, with the writer having to sit cross-legged behind it.

I must confess that I thought then that my inner-city family and I had very little in common, though their undemanding, non-competitive nature made them unusually comfortable to be with. What attracted me there was the food, which was uncommon, and, of course, witnessing my mother's relaxed pleasure at being 'home'. As in Kanpur, she seemed to be in control of her own life once again, falling into the pace of her childhood with ease. Veena and I would climb the narrow stairs to the roof. From here we could hear the hum of the city. If we spun around, our eyes could look down on family life in hundreds of courtyards that became ever-smaller as they stretched into the distance. If we looked straight ahead in a southeasterly direction, our gaze would meet the grand dome and minarets of Jama Masjid, the seventeenth-century mosque. We could hear all the calls to prayer. Meanwhile, my mother changed into her cottons and settled down to knit, hem or attach a border to a saree – she rarely sat idly – and to catch up with family news.

There were few servants in this household and the cooking was done mostly by my aunt, my mother's brother's wife, though all the women and girls pitched in, scraping bitter gourds, shelling green chickpeas and pinching off small fenugreek leaves. My sister and I were rarely allowed to join in as we were considered 'guests'. We hung around, unable to tear ourselves away from the aromas.

One of the specialities of the house was a sauced dish of monsoon mushrooms. I never had them as good anywhere else. These were not the common white mushrooms now sold all over Delhi, though they were white in colour. Called *khumbi*, they consisted of very slight, three-inch, edible stems topped with elongated, narrow caps that closed in on themselves so no gills were visible. These mushrooms chose to spring out of the earth only when the rains poured during the monsoon season. They were so delicate – and expensive – that they were sold in baskets, heaped into little piles. Their texture was smooth and satiny, not unlike that of the fresh straw mushrooms I have since eaten only in the Far East.

My aunt, Mainji, with her large protruding teeth, knew how to cook them to perfection. She always said, 'There is nothing to it.' There must have been *something* to it because even my mother's *khumbi* was not quite like hers.

Mainji would take off her shoes, step into the kitchen and squat on the floor in front of a brazier, blowing on the charcoal until it glowed to her liking. A pot would go on top of the coal, then some oil and the cooking began. The mushrooms took but ten minutes and seemed to require only cumin, coriander, turmeric and chilli powder, but in some magical proportion that she alone had mastered. She prepared one dish after another. There was meat – all the men in her family required it just as those in ours did – and several seasonal vegetables, one more delicious than the next: tiny stuffed bitter gourds, okra with dried green mango, green chickpeas cooked in a pilaf, and pumpkin cooked with fennel seeds.

The *pièce de résistance*, for me at any rate, were the mushrooms. But would I get to eat any? Lunch was served quite late and the men were always served first. Striped *durees* were spread out on a shady end of the courtyard, topped with a fresh white sheet. The men took off their shoes and sat down in a circle. The women served them, placing all the food in the centre.

I would watch the mushrooms disappear, wondering if there would be any left for us. As the men served themselves generously, I would hold my breath. When it was our turn to eat, there were fewer mushrooms and more sauce. By that time I hardly cared. The sauce was delicious too. I scooped it up with bits of my poori and just devoured it.

After lunch some grown-ups napped while others sat in groups and talked. My sister and I went up and down the stairs, in and out of all the rooms, breaking off and eating a leaf of holy basil (*tulsi*) whenever we passed the plant near the prayer room.

For tea, Mainji sent out for some roasted white sweet potatoes (*shakarkandi*), some star fruit (*kumruq*) and some roasted water chestnuts (*singharas*). These she made into a spicy *chaat* to serve with our sweet, milky tea. It was then time to leave. My mother gathered up her needlework, freshened up and changed back into her silks. *Attachee* case and handbag in hand, we walked out of her family portals. We always returned a different way, partly because of where the car could park and partly because my mother still had some unfinished business in the Tinsel Bazaar (*Kinari Bazaar*) and in

Dariba, the Street of Jewellers. In the first she picked up spice mixes like *chaat masala* from a speciality stall that has existed in the same spot for all of my life, and in the latter she checked on pieces of jewellery that she always seemed to have on order, bangles, rings and necklaces. We made our last stop right at the end of Dariba, just where it met the main street, *Chandni Chowk*. This was at the shop that sold *jalebis*, the squiggly, pretzel-like sweets filled with syrup. We liked them hot and crisp, straight out of the wok and freshly dunked in syrup. The *jalebis* would be served to us on a leaf, which we would carry to our car. Our sticky hands and mouths would be quite busy during the journey home.

CHAPTER EIGHTEEN

Learning to Swim and Dance ❋ *A Haven for Musicians*
Temple Dancers and Tap-dancers ❋ *Dressing as Milkmaids*
An Unhappy Teenager ❋ *The Drama of the Monsoons*
Shibbudada's Quiet Cruelty ❋ *The Spring Festival of Colours*

I was settling into my life in Delhi. My father had joined the Chelmsford Club, whose only advantage for me was its swimming pool. Most weekends, Rajesh and I would hop onto a bus at Alipur Road and slowly make our way there. He would disappear into the men's changing room while I went into the ladies', then we'd meet to jump into the pool. Here he continued his swimming lessons, teaching me how to float and then to do the crawl. With my thin, weak ankles and wrists, I was indifferent at all sports. My body lacked muscular tone and strength. Physically, I was a weakling. At school, I had already been nicknamed the dreaded 'bookworm'. The only strength I possessed lay in my single-mindedness and dogged determination. The brain just pulled the body along. I not only managed to learn how to swim but to love being in the water as well. I still do.

Something similar had happened with dance. Because of Shibbudada's deep love for Indian classical music, Number 7 had turned into a haven for India's foremost singers and musicians. Shibbudada was an old-fashioned patron of the arts who spent his money supporting his passions. The artists were encouraged to stay with us, evenings were set up for private recitals and all of Delhi's music-loving glitterati invited to attend.

Some summer evenings, if there was a full moon and the light reflecting off the Yamuna River could add its own special brilliance, the recitals were held on the roof but normally they were in the drawing room. Overstuffed chairs and sofas were pushed against the wall and large white sheets spread across the Persian carpet for most people to sit on. A special area was set up at the fireplace end for the musician of the day to sit like a monarch – on the floor, of course – and pour out his enchantment. These recitals generally started after dinner. Musicians preferred to start late and then, if they were inspired enough, play into the early hours of the morning, ending with morning ragas. Tea, cigarettes, whisky, juices, ice cream and betel leaves were served during the recitals. It was considered *déclassé* to interrupt the music for anything else.

At Number 7, music teachers had always been available to anyone wishing to avail of them. I couldn't sing at all and gave up early. My older sisters, who had sweet voices and could carry a tune, had been cast in every convent musical. I had given up on the theatre after an early stint at the age of five as the Brown Mouse in the *Pied Piper of Hamelin*. St Mary's Convent in Kanpur performed only musicals and I was no good at them. Out of all my grandfather's grandchildren, the most musical turned out to be the three Shibbudada had produced.

They were angrily, passionately musical. Raghudada, the eldest son, played the violin. He would end up as a renowned statistician at Chicago University but his love of both classical Indian and Western music would continue throughout his life. Indeed, when my American husband, then a violinist with the New York Philharmonic, visited India, it was Raghudada who guided him in his purchases of classical Indian recordings. Rajesh, the youngest, played the *tabla* (drums). Sheila sang. Sheila may have reminded her father of her mother in her looks but he must surely have been startled by her singing. He began to notice her for the first time.

Shibbudada's interest in music had not extended to dance but one year, when I was thirteen, a South Indian troupe that performed temple dances was to perform in Delhi for the first time. Bharata Natyam was an energetic, devotional form of dancing that North India had never before seen. The unknown dancers and their troupe leader, Ram Gopal, needed a place to stay and Number 7 was offered. I saw them practise each day and was entranced. I fell in love with Bharata Natyam.

It just so happened that some American tap-dancers were staying with us at the same time. At Number 7, a system of open hospitality was the norm. Poor relatives and artists (who were generally equally poor) could stay as long as they wished. One blind uncle – I never did understand exactly how he was related to us – came to us with his five daughters and didn't leave until each of his daughters had been married off on our premises. Counting his blessings, he had married off two of them at one go. He lived in the room I once used for my Hindi lessons.

One magical summer night, while the Bharata Natyam troupe was still staying with us, we youngsters were all sitting outside on a lawn perfumed heavily with jasmine and Queen of the Night flowers. All those of my parents' generation were in bed. An American tap-dancer, speaking to a South Indian drum (*mridangam*) player, said, 'I'm sure I can tap to any rhythm you can play,' to which the *mridangam* player replied, 'And I'm sure I can play anything you can tap.' And so began a night of friendly, East–West competition that was to last until dawn. This was around 1945–6, well before Yehudi Menuhin came to India and any rapport between Eastern and Western music had been established. The large *takht* (divan) outside was cleared of its mattress and sheets, exposing the bare wood, and the two 'competitors' jumped on top. It was an exhilarating, inspiring night. As the two goaded each other towards even more complicated rhythms and greater glory, I knew in my heart that I just had to learn to dance.

And I did. Unfortunately, no-one in the Delhi of that time could teach me Bharata Natyam. I had to settle for one of the two styles performed commonly in North India: Kathak, a dance form that developed in the Moghul court; and Manipuri, a soft, rhythmic, almost folk form that had developed in the far-eastern Indian state of Manipur.

In the end, I learned both, one in school and the other through a private teacher at home. Once again, I was plagued by a lack of strength and stamina but learned enough to perform in minor recitals and to love dance forever.

For my first public dance recital, a school friend, Promela, and I were to do a duet in the Manipuri form. What should we wear? I suggested we dress as local milkmaids. I, for one, knew exactly what they wore. After all, I crossed the Yamuna River in the same wooden boat they used, and many of them came to work in Number 7's cowshed or could be seen squatting on the lawns, weeding and cutting our grass with scythes in the monsoon season. They were visions of beauty, with their top-knotted hair over which they flung a bright veil that fell to the back; their short, equally bright, forty-yard skirts (very full, gathered skirts made with forty yards of material) that came to mid-calf; and their masses of silver jewellery that covered their wrists, arms, ankles, necks and hair. These were our local village women. Much of their personal wealth was in the silver they wore about their bodies.

We started to dress for our recital. I opened up the large bundle of silver loot I had borrowed from our own, rather large *gwalan* (female cowherd). As I began putting it on, Promela ventured a quiet remark: 'Are you sure you can dance with so much jewellery?' 'Of course I can,' I replied, determined to dazzle. I danced well enough. But as I spun and flung my arms around, first my bracelets, then my anklets – all too large for my thin bones – began to fly off, one at a time. As we danced faster, there were bracelets flying all over the stage. I hardly knew if I should stop and retrieve them, carry on, stepping on the jewellery as I did, or fall down in a heap and burst into tears. I carried on but wept buckets at my own foolishness as soon as I was home.

Twelve and thirteen were not easy ages for me. I was struggling at school and, without my older sisters, struggling at home. There was no niche I fitted into with any comfort. I was not pretty, I excelled at nothing and sighed a lot. Quite naturally, I had developed pathetic crushes on my cousins' friends, all to no purpose as I was too shy to say anything. I spent my time wrapping myself around Number 7's elegant white pillars and moping or weeping. The monsoon season in particular brought out all my deepest despair.

Monsoons in India are a romantic time. Just as Western literature suggests that it is with the arrival of spring that all thoughts turn to love, Indian literature, music, local customs and even food all make a similar case for the monsoon season. With good reason.

Veena plays in the well-equipped garden at Number 7.
Part of the annexe is in the background.

The monsoons arrive with such drama, especially in the north. The summer starts in April with the hot, *loo* desert winds blowing hot air and sand with cruel ferocity. Temperatures rise to 104 or 105 degrees Fahrenheit. If you get into a car, the leather burns your skin; if you touch metal, you get a rash or blister. The trees are subjected daily to thick coatings of dust; the grass turns brown and starts to disappear; the earth cakes and cracks. You drink cooling green mango juice or lime juice with salt, sugar or both, or try to decompress with the juice from the watermelon rind pickles that sit in large, round terracotta pots. Nothing cools you down for long.

My sister Veena and I would run the distance between Number 5 and Number 7 in the summers as if demons were chasing us. Number 5 had air conditioners. Number 7 had thick vetiver (*khas*) curtains on the outside of every door or window that were kept constantly wet. Hot winds blowing through them magically cooled down, picking up the remarkable perfume of these prized roots as they did so. But between Numbers 5 and 7 there was only a boiling hell.

The summer seemed endless. It went on through May, June and part of July. Eating mangoes came and went as did cherries from Kashmir and lychees from Dehradun. Summer vegetable gardens yielded only soft marrows and squashes, the bowling pin-like *ghiyas*, the tennis ball-shaped *tindas*, and the slightly glutinous *toris*, and we tired of them easily. The earth and sky remained broiling and menacing. After lunch we all tried sleeping through the long hot afternoons. There was a *takht* (divan) covered by a giant white sheet (*chandini*) in the big, east-facing room at Number 7. With pillows placed all down its centre, it was large enough to sleep about twenty people lying alongside each other, ten to a side. But our sleep was restless as chirping birds, seeking respite in all our verandahs, kept up a noisy chatter.

Then one day, quite suddenly, there was a change in the air. A hint of some momentous possibility went through it like an electric charge, even though the heat remained. Dark clouds began appearing on the horizon. Majestic and threatening, like a dark army on the move, they got closer and closer. We all rushed to the verandah and began to inhale that anticipated smell of freshly wet earth that Indians have tried to capture in an *attar* called, rather simply, 'earth' (*mitti*). It was a faraway smell, almost as if we were imagining it. Soon the entire sky was dark with black clouds. Thunder boomed from all sides, accompanied by zigzags of lightning. The earth seemed hotter than ever. First one or two fat drops of rain fell, then more and more until there was a deluge. Suddenly the heat broke as if some shell encasing us had been cracked open. We all rushed out onto the paved driveway just outside Number 7's front verandah, held our faces up to the sky and allowed ourselves to get thoroughly soaked. The monsoon season had finally arrived. We could now feast on monsoon sweets – squiggly, pretzel-shaped *jabelis*, full of syrup – dunking them in glasses of cold milk as we gazed dreamily at the downpour.

The first cooling breezes went through the hearts of most young people, awakening or intensifying their yearnings and joys. Whether we were just following the suggestions of an ancient tradition that proclaimed the monsoon season to be the most 'romantic' one, or whether there really was a collection of elements that provoked and egged on the romantic spirit, is hard to say. All I know is that around the ages of twelve and thirteen I was a self-conscious, bespectacled bundle of misery and the monsoon just made it worse. It set before me all the possibilities without offering any hope.

There was nothing in school that interested me enough. I did well by dint of hard work but my heart was not in it. I knew, I just knew that a world existed into which I would fit some day. It just wasn't the world I was in right then. Boys I had crushes on, boys at the swimming pool, completely ignored me, mostly because I couldn't summon up the nerve to say one word to them. The irony was that I wasn't really shy. I could be quite bold when I wanted to be. I lacked tact and softness, was too much a mixture of insecurity and arrogance to flirt, and had the awful habit of watching and instantly analysing myself and all others around me so that I allowed no action to be entirely carefree or spontaneous.

Shibbudada – whose validation, however contrary that seemed, we all craved – did not seem to care much, but he did notice. Once he complained, 'Why are your eyes so dull? At your age they should be shining like that of a wild animal, like those of your cousin D—.'

I wanted to shout back, 'But cousin D— does not read all day or write all day or THINK. Cousin D— is an idiot.' But I said nothing. Cousin D— was pretty. I was overcome with insecurity.

At another time during the winter, I just happened to be sitting by the fire in the drawing room next to Shibbudada when my boy cousins walked in with a particularly good-looking friend. My heart began to beat so fast, I thought it would pop out of my mouth. To cover my confusion, I turned away towards Shibbudada and started up some innocuous conversation, but he saw right through me and stopped me in my tracks, saying, 'You don't really want to talk to me right now. Why don't you keep your eyes where your interest really lies?' I could have died of shame and inadequacy.

As I grew older, I began to tolerate Shibbudada's behaviour less and less. He sensed this and started to return the favour with a regimen of quiet cruelty. He demanded nothing short of adoration and I was not providing it. Always in two minds about him, Shibbudada's children seemed to be getting ever more prickly, contrary and unpredictable. I never uttered a word against their father to them, particularly to Rajesh who was my friend, as I suspected it would only lead to a spirited defence. I could never talk to my parents or brothers and sisters about him as they all seemed to either adore or forgive Shibbudada much more easily than I could. I berated myself endlessly for being hard-hearted and not 'deserving' and 'good' like my sisters Kamal and Lalit. Even in our very large joint family where we were rarely, physically, alone, I felt very alone.

(I have now, almost sixty years later, found out that I had company. As I was going around collecting old photographs from cousins for this book, we began recounting old times and I discovered that Shibbudada had tormented most of them. 'You too? You too?' I said to each one of them in disbelief. He was their god too, family-anointed and permanent. They had all hungered for his approval, just like me, and hardly ever received it. They too had been subjected to the games he played with his favours and his power. What if we had just talked to each other? None of us knew what the others were feeling. For some reason, we had all held our separate tongues.)

To add to my woes, I soon came down with a severe case of chicken pox. This happened at Holi, the spring festival of colours. We had always celebrated our Holi holidays in Delhi, even when we were living in Kanpur. The women of the house would start off the Holi season with the preparation of *bara* pickles. These were rather like Jewish cucumber pickles except, instead of cucumbers, it was dumplings that were pickled in a spicy brine flecked with plenty of crushed mustard seeds.

These were uncommon pickles. We knew no other community that pickled dumplings. But we did, and delicious they were too. *Urad dal*, the most ancient of Indian legumes, was soaked, seasoned, ground into a paste, beaten to allow the infiltration of air bubbles, and then formed into patties on a piece of muslin with a wetted hand. Each patty was carefully transferred to a *karhai* (wok) filled with hot oil and fried before it was dropped into the pickling solution. The combination of liquid and dumplings was then ladled into *mutkas*, round-bottomed terracotta pots with narrow necks. These were covered with lids and left in Number 7's northern court-yard on wooden stands to 'mature' in the sun. If my grandmother, who gave it a swish and a taste now and then, declared that it was not quite ready, it just meant that it had not soured sufficiently for her taste.

Once the *baras* were firmly ensconced in their brine, the family's collective attention turned to other Holi foods: there were *papris*, crisp, chickpea flour 'poppadums', nicely spiced but hard to roll out as the dough needed to be really hard; *goojas*, turnovers filled with coconut and sweetened nuts; and of course there were those *pakoris*, fritters that had to be made at the last minute. These were not ordinary fritters. These were laced with *bhang*, or hash.

There were aspects of my life in India that, in retrospect, seem difficult to reconcile. We were a conservative, buttoned-down Kayastha family but with forward-looking, intellectually liberal leanings. We could question anything we wanted to and did. But we followed family Hindu traditions to the letter, almost by rote, as if they were some form of incessant background rhythm. We even took full advantage of the licence these traditions allowed on certain days without much thought, such as gambling at Diwali so that the clinking of money would entice the goddess of wealth into our homes.

At Holi, tradition suggested that both sexes throw inhibition to the winds, mingle freely, sprinkle coloured waters and powders on each other, dance, sing, and yes, for the adults, drink alcohol and even partake of hash. The couplet we chanted with some frequency on Holi day, '*Kahay, sunay ka bura na mano, Aaj humari Holi hai*' could be translated as, 'Don't be offended by anything we say or do, For today is our Holi'. For one day in the year, we had been 'freed'.

Holi's origins probably lay in India's distant pantheistic past when the spring harvest must have been celebrated with a certain abandon. In India, a tradition is rarely lost; rather it acquires layers through the years. We still recognized its harvest-time beginnings. On the night before Holi we built a bonfire and threw into it sheaves of newly picked wheat from our faraway farms and, better still, sheaves of freshly harvested chickpea stalks. As soon as they had roasted sufficiently, we dragged them out with long poles and fell upon them, separating the wheat grains and peas from their blackened skins. Our fingers and mouths turned sooty as we ate but we could not stop munching until the last chickpea had been found and devoured.

The next day we played Holi. Preparations for the 'playing' had already begun. The *mali* (gardener) had scrubbed out the cement water tank in the garden, plugged it and filled it with about two-and-a-half feet of water. Into the water were emptied several baskets of dried *tesu* flowers which, when soaked, released a yellowish-orange dye and a pleasantly musky aroma. The flowers floated to the top, swelled and, looking rather like large bumble bees, covered the surface of the water.

The children's preparations were less benign. First, we made sure that all the *gulaal*, the coloured powders, had been ordered, the reds our parents preferred and the more vile and new-fangled yellows, greens, blues and purples that we liked. Then, we went into the garage and asked Babaji's driver, Masoom Ali, for the darkest grease he had lying about. He tried to put us off with, 'You children are always eating my head. Go away. Don't bother me.' But in the end he always relented. The grease was put into jars and reserved for those we disliked. And for those we liked or even loved? Ah, there was the gold powder that was carefully mixed with oil and hidden in a special spot from where it could be whisked out to transform the faces of the desired ones into those of gods and goddesses.

We awoke at dawn on Holi day, made sure our brass water-squirters were ready for ambush and pails of coloured water and powders hidden strategically. The first people to be attacked and overwhelmed were all the cousins themselves. We had already planned our moves. As our parents shouted, 'Not inside the house, go out, Holi must be played outside the house,' we tackled each other and were not content until we were all fully wet, had received a dunking in the *tesu* tank and had our faces smeared with a variety of powders.

Once we had finished with each other – the elders got a politer version of the treatment – old and young gathered on Number 7's driveway to march to all the neighbouring houses. Each household was equally prepared and gave as good as it got. Everywhere we went we were offered food and drink, the same *papris, goojas, bara* pickles, whisky and the hash-laced drinks and fritters. Our numbers and raucousness increased as members of households we had attacked joined us. We ended up in Number 7, a few hundred of us, sitting under the jujube tree on the front lawn. A harmonium and a set of *tablas* (drums) were brought out, and the singing and dancing began. '*Holi ayee ray kanha, Bruj kay basiya*,' we sang. These were mostly hymn-like, mediaeval songs about Lord Krishna playing Holi with the milkmaids – hymn-like and lusty.

I remember this particular Holi when I was exactly twelve-and-a-half years old, neither child nor woman, my hair smeared with green and purple, my face golden and my body wet with *tesu* water, an unrecognizable creature shivering on the grass under the jujube tree. My head was aching, I remember, aching so it felt as if it might explode. Everything had gone into slow motion. I remember someone turning towards me and saying, 'Who is she? She looks quite pretty.' I wanted to explain, 'It's only the gold paint. This is me. I don't have my glasses on.' My mouth opened to speak and then shut again without uttering a word. Then my parents got up and started dancing. I must have begun to fade away for the next thing I heard was my brother, Bhaiyyadada's, voice, 'Are you all right? You seem feverish.'

Bhaiyyadada walked me to Number 5 where I had a quick bath and crawled into bed. Big blisters had begun appearing – on my face, my arms, my body – I had a severe case of chicken pox.

CHAPTER NINETEEN

Chicken Pox ❋ Soup-toast and Sewing
A Fancy-dress Party

The chicken pox lasted a good three weeks. I was convinced I would come out of it severely deformed as many of the blisters had filled up with pus and some were a good three-quarters of an inch in diameter. No-one was allowed to visit: I was completely quarantined. The blisters first hurt, then itched, never allowing me to lie in comfort. My father's eldest sister, Bhuaji, offered me little food packets over the Number 5 wall filled with *mutthries* (savoury biscuits). I devoured these quickly with thick layers of my grandmother's *meethi* chutney (sweet chutney made with shredded green mangoes and ginger). One good thing that came of this long illness was that our family began eating all its meals in Number 5. Our much smaller kitchen was humming all day and we were ecstatic.

My mother, whose calm ministrations had so comforted my father during all his minor illnesses, now turned her full attention to me, but her tactics were entirely different. Besides spoon-feeding me 'soup-toast' – simple chicken and meat broths with slices of toast for dunking, which I loved – she approached me with another of her talents. She began teaching me how to sew. She had already taught me knitting when I was five. By now I was knitting the most complicated designs, many of my own devising, requiring several colours that snaked their way across and up the insides of cardigans, vests and pullovers.

Sewing was another matter. We had a tailor, Ram Narain, to do the simple stuff. He came to us from the Old City on a bicycle and worked at one end of the Number 5 dining room for weeks at a time. We bought the fabrics and sketched out the designs. He sat on the floor on a mat with my mother's Singer sewing machine and did his best to interpret our thoughts. If there was a wedding on the horizon, he stayed for months. He irritated us because he never followed our designs to the letter and because his finishing was hurried and careless. His buttons were never aligned and his hemming was slipshod. Besides, he always cut the thread with his teeth. My mother kept reminding us that any help was hard to find and that we should be grateful to have him at all.

I considered myself highly stylish and was not content with Ram Narain's bumbling approach. There were no ready-made clothes in India then so with my mother's expert help, my chicken pox days were happily employed with sewing. In this period I made two *kameezes* (shirts) to go on top of the *shalwars* (baggy trousers) we wore. One was a delicate white poplin with a turtle neck and the second was a cream silk. The first I boldly embroidered with an anchor placed just above the left breast. A 'rope', which I made by twisting some silk threads, wound around the anchor, going in and out of the white poplin through strategically placed buttonholes. The second shirt had a much more elaborate piece of embroidery in the same spot above the left breast. It consisted of the ace, king and queen of hearts fanned out prettily.

Heartened by my skills, I began preparing for my thirteenth birthday in the coming August. It would be a fancy-dress party and I would think up and design something really grand. Cousins and friends were duly informed. Everyone's dress was a secret. Enthusiasm poured in from all quarters, even from Shibbudada. He

*My thirteenth birthday. The party consisted mostly of cousins with
the honourable exception of my friend, Sudha (front row, third from right), and
two of Sheila's friends. Fancy dress was the order of the day.*

insisted there be a photographer to cover the event. He would
arrange for one. My birthday would be held in Number 7, he said.

Suddenly the stakes had got higher than I wanted and I was
nervous. I still didn't have anything to wear. I thought up and rejected
idea after idea. It was already early August before I settled on being
a hula girl with a grass skirt and a short blouse. The blouse seemed
easy enough. I already had decently large breasts. I would wear a
white blouse and tuck it up so my waist was visible and my breasts
defined. The skirt I would make. I would cut up hundreds of strips
of paper and sew them on to a waistband. My hair? My hair was
long and I would just leave it loose.

The day dawned and I began to dress. I put on the blouse. It
looked like just an ordinary blouse. I rolled it up at the waist but it

kept rolling down, and the bulk hid all definition of my newly formed breasts. There was no time to worry about that. I tied on the skirt. Every time I moved a few of the paper strips tore off. I undid my two long braids and combed out my hair. I still looked just like myself, not like a hula girl at all. I cried. My mother insisted that I looked just fine and that I hurry on to Number 7 before the guests arrived.

My cousins and friends came, girls dressed as boys, boys dressed as girls. There were Arabs with daggers, Japanese damsels with fans and milkmaids with a ton of silver jewellery. I blew out the candles on my cake from Wengers, helped pass along the slabs of three-in-one (chocolate, strawberry and vanilla) Kwality ice cream and nibbled on the spicy samosas from Ghantaywallah in Chandni Chowk. Finally, I posed in the centre of my group birthday photograph. But my heart was not in any of it.

CHAPTER TWENTY

*Learning to Fly * School Days in Summer * Mrs McKelvie*
*Discovering Drama * Fearless Amina * Art Appreciation*

I think it was around the time of my thirteenth birthday that I started growing up. School, Queen Mary's, helped. I was out of Middle School and Hindi was no longer the medium of instruction. Even though I had mastered it, I felt easier with the English we would use through the upper classes. Instead of plodding, I could now fly. The school, a dour, grey-stone building with gothic arches, had been modernized.

The summers had been quite unbearable until then as none of the classrooms were equipped with electric ceiling fans. The shirts we wore on top of our *shalwars* (baggy pants) didn't help either. Even if made from the thinnest voiles, they didn't stop the perspiration from running down our bodies and legs. When we picked up our pens to write, sweat trickled down our arms and over our pens onto the notebooks. The pens slithered about in our fingers. Wearing all white did little to inspire a sense of cool wellbeing in that stone school building.

What the school did provide to all classes were cloth pulley fans. Imagine, if you will, a long rod or beam suspended near the ceiling above the length of a classroom, almost bisecting it. Imagine a curtain with many pleats, about two-and-a-half feet in length, hanging from the full length of this rod. Now imagine a simple pulley system attached to the rod that allows someone to pull the entire contraption back and forth, thus 'fanning' the whole classroom as a hand-held fan might. Ingenious? The operative words, of course, are 'someone' and 'hand-held'.

The 'someones' the school hired were our local village women who came to their fanning jobs every day wearing their bright forty-yard skirts, provocative, brassiere-sized blouses and head-to-toe silver jewellery. Their job was to take the pulley rope in their hands, extend it through the classroom door to the verandah just outside it, sit down on the verandah floor and start pulling and releasing, pulling and releasing.

The first few pulls were quite exciting. But the weight of their clothing, the sheer boredom of their job and the numbing heat slowly lulled the women into ever slower and then non-existent motion. First they could be seen half-sitting, then half-lying down, then lying down and pulling the rope with their toes, then lying down and snoring. Every now and then one of my schoolmates would give the rope a tug which would waken them briefly, but to no long-term purpose.

We would rush out for a drink between classes but the only water we could get was from the tap at a small tank in the courtyard. We cupped a hand and drank it straight from the source. It was always too warm and offered no respite.

There was one bit of relief though. Everyday at mid-morning, there was – if we signed up and paid for it in advance – a break for '*do phal, do biscuit*' or 'two fruits, two biscuits'. The English school nurse, in full uniform, dispensed these from a special table, checking us against her list as she did so.

I was always in two minds about signing up as I did not care for biscuits (having lost my sweet tooth in Daurala), and the fruit was always a mediocre orange and an unripe banana, the only variation being two mediocre oranges or two unripe bananas. What I really loved, and what I could have only if I splurged on the biscuits and fruit, was a glass of cold, cold milk.

This was no ordinary milk. It didn't come straight from the cow's udders like ours did at home. It hadn't been boiled in a kitchen pot and cooled. No, this was homogenized milk from a proper dairy and came in a glass bottle. I just loved it. Sometimes I paid for the whole package just to get the milk but most of the time I gave up as the fruit was not even good enough to give away and ended up rotting slowly inside my desk.

It must have dawned on the school at some stage that pulley fans were a losing proposition. By the time I was thirteen, they had been replaced by ceiling fans.

Many of the teachers had been replaced too. I was blessed with Mrs McKelvie, a Parsi lady of about the same height as I was, perhaps even shorter. She was married to a Briton, which accounted for her name. With a sweet, round, light-skinned face and brown hair that she wore as a braided wreath around her head, she could easily have passed for an Englishwoman. In a school where there were both English and Indian personnel at that time, she wore only sarees to class (though with European blouses), so there would be no mistaking who she really was. She wore her sarees oddly though, as if she had lived in England too long. What struck me when I first saw her was the combination of her laughing, intelligent eyes and her small, even teeth, which were caked with nicotine.

Mrs McKelvie was my history teacher. She didn't teach me just Indian and British history, which were part of the set curriculum, but that any subject could be fascinating if I delved into it deeply enough. She showed me how history could be researched from a hundred angles, some obscure and seemingly unrelated; that the study and drawing of maps led to ever greater clarity; that understanding the character of emperors and generals was sometimes as important as the dates of their battles. She wanted me to read everything: *1066 and All That*, Shakespeare's plays, Emperor Akbar's biography by Abul Fazl, Nehru's books written in jail where the British had imprisoned him. She wanted me to see everything: the Red Fort in Delhi, the paintings of Turner, Moghul miniature paintings, Buddhist art. Because I loved drawing she set me to work making monstrous maps that the school then framed and hung up in the library.

When the school decided to stage a performance of Shakespeare's *A Midsummer Night's Dream*, she suggested my name for the role of Titania, Queen of the Fairies. Titania – and Shakespeare – opened up the possibilities of a future I did not think I had, or deserved. Here I was, floating outdoors on the lovely grass stage of Queen Mary's School, eyes outlined with black, lips a luscious scarlet, body swathed in green, shimmering robes, declaiming in righteous anger to a slippery Fairy King:

> These are the forgeries of jealousy;
> And never, since the middle summer's spring,
> Met we on hill, in dale, forest, or mead,
> By paved fountain or by rushy brook,
> Or in the beached margent of the sea,
> To dance our ringlets to the whistling wind,
> But with thy brawls thou hast disturbed our sport.

I felt elated and at home. Every atom of my being felt energized and utilized. My cup, suddenly, was full. That constant critical chatter in my head stopped. Whatever was missing in me had been completed. I was consumed with purpose.

I knew enough to say 'pave-ed' and 'beach-ed'. Another new and excellent teacher, Miss Dutt who taught us English, had just covered the iambic pentameter so I was prepared for Shakespearean niceties. Besides, the college of my grandfather, father, aunts and now my brothers, St Stephen's College, performed at least one Shakespeare play every winter for as long as I could remember. Not only could I be found in the front row, year after year, but I was also known for my firm opinions on the performances, such as that of Joyce Christian as Rosalind. Joyce, a tall, shapely Anglo-Indian, was one of the few women at St Stephen's. The college seemed unable to decide whether it wanted women pupils or not, reversing its decision every other year. Joyce got in during one of the 'yes' periods but was in a very small minority. All the boys were half in love with her and so was I, especially when she was on the stage.

When I was asked to play the lead in *Robin Hood and his Merry Men* at school, I was ready for that too. Already a half-boy since early childhood, I donned my tights and tunic with glee, picked up my bow and arrow and entered the fray in Sherwood Forest as if I had been born in Nottingham.

There were other infusions to the blood. Out of the haze that separated juniors from those in more senior classes, one face kept asserting its presence. It belonged to a girl about three or four years older than me called Amina Ahmed. For someone like me who came from a staid family of fully-documented ancestors, a family in which kind married kind, Amina's history was enviable, and she

repeated it with a certain pride. She was a Muslim girl from the inner
city whose father was the illegitimate son of a prostitute. It couldn't
get much better than that!

But it did. This father, Nuruddin Ahmed, had managed to
educate himself enough to become a lawyer, and when in England
met and married a half-Jewish woman named Bertha Boam, commonly known as Billy. Amina was the offspring of this unusual
couple who still lived in the inner city near a disreputable movie
house we had been warned to avoid, Novelty Cinema. She was as
blonde and light-skinned as her mother and sported her father's
long, prominent nose. She wore her silky blonde hair in a fashionable pageboy. Quite fearless, she could out-swear any local ruffian in
street lingo but also spoke the most chaste, elegant Urdu when it
was required. (Later, as the wife of an Indian ambassador, she was
to master Russian and Persian as well.) None of the Anglican super-
visors in our school could control or suppress her.

Miss Devi Ditta, our principal, tried. Each morning started with
an assembly of all the students for prayers. Here we stood in rows
according to the class we were in, with the younger children standing in front. We began with hymns, accompanied by nurse on the
piano. These were Christian hymns, but because most of us were
Hindus, Muslims and Sikhs, certain concessions were made. Instead
of singing, 'Onward Christian soldiers' we sang, 'Onward, onward
soldiers'. I did not realize until I heard my father-in-law singing in a
Brooklyn church some decades later that our words in India had
been altered. After hymns and prayers, announcements were made
about trips to inter-school games or '*chaat* parties' to raise money for
a charity, or about new teachers. This was followed by a cursory
'inspection' to check that our clothing was neat, our hair tidy and
free of lice, and our nails clean and unpolished.

It was absolutely forbidden to use nail polish. Amina's nails, short and bitten, were nonetheless always polished, varnished a bright red or pink. Her name would be called out, a common occurrence.

'Amina Ahmed!' Miss Devi Ditta would say in an exasperated voice, 'You have been asked again and again not to wear nail polish. Kindly go with nurse and remove it.'

AMINA: 'I can't.'

MISS DEVI DITTA: 'What do you mean you can't?'

AMINA: 'I can't. I am not allowed.'

MISS DEVI DITTA: 'Who is not allowing you?'

AMINA: 'Doctor's orders. I have to keep the nail polish on to protect my nails.'

MISS DEVI DITTA: 'I have never heard of such nonsense.'

AMINA: 'I have shimiitis [or some other invented name]. If I remove the nail polish my nails will fall off.'

And so Amina would get away with it again. I would stare back at her and invoke my Hindu gods in awe. My admiration for her knew no bounds.

Amina behaved with equal gumption in the drawing class. Not that she and I went to the same class but I knew the drill. Miss Aloo MacAdam, the art teacher, taught only two things – object drawing and painting – and in the same way year after year.

For object drawing she placed one or two wooden blocks, and perhaps a bottle or a vase with flowers as well, at the front of the class on a table. We sat in semicircular rows at a little distance with our drawing books open on our desks, well-sharpened pencils beside them, and drew the objects.

In order to get the proportions right, we had to keep measuring. 'Hold your pencil out in front of you. Keep it straight. Close one eye. Now measure the length of the box on your pencil. Mark that point. Now measure the height of the box. Mark that. On your pencil, how many times does the height go into the length? Follow those proportions. Then use your watercolours and paint the objects in. Use the colours you actually see, making them paler where light hits the objects.'

I had no trouble with any of this because I could draw and paint anyway. Miss MacAdam's directions only helped me double-check what my natural instincts already knew. She always rewarded me with the highest marks and showed my work around as an example.

Somehow, it was not enough. I needed Amina's approval. I had heard that she was an 'artist', so one day I waited for her outside the art room, drawing book in hand.

It took a while for her to come out. Most of her class had already left when she and Miss MacAdam emerged. Miss MacAdam looked cross. Amina looked nonchalant. Miss MacAdam went back into the art room and banged the door shut behind her.

'Amina,' I said, 'I want to show you my drawing.'

She looked at it.

'What do you think?' I persisted.

'Do *you* like it?' she asked me. 'The most important thing is that you should like it.'

I was suddenly insecure. Unsure. 'May I see what you did in class,' I managed.

She held out her drawing book. She had broken up her blocks, bowl and vase into bits and pieces, scattering them about her page, and then coloured them in nail polish colours: magentas, reds, fuchsias and oranges. The objects and colours were unrecognizable, that is, if you tried to match them to anything real in the art room, but the painting was beautiful.

Here was another dawn, another awakening. West European painters of the late nineteenth and early twentieth century had already left their mark on us. On one of my birthdays, my family had given me a book of the paintings of European masters. I would sit with this heavy tome in my lap, drinking in the images on its thick, glossy pages day after day. Rembrandt, Holbein and Da Vinci were there but so were the more fragmented, angular worlds of Cézanne and Picasso. Just below this book, on the same shelf, I kept a thinner volume containing the turn-of-the-century paintings of Jamini Roy. A Bengali, he painted stylized folk-arty figures in few strokes and bright colours. This too was well-thumbed. My favourite painter though, whose work I loved with a passion then, was Amrita Sher-Gil, a half-Indian, half-Hungarian woman who had studied in France in the early 1930s, returned to India and died at 29, but not before leaving the most graceful images of fluid Indian figures, often draped in striped clothing.

Until then, I had never been to an exhibition of paintings and did not apply the lessons I might have learnt from my art books to myself. I admired the freedom of painters but did not realize that the freedom could apply to me, even at the age of thirteen, even while I was a mere student. In the end, I was not as bold as Amina. I painted as Miss MacAdam wanted me to in the art room but bought myself some oils and painted in furious blobs at home.

CHAPTER TWENTY-ONE

The Sisters Return ❀ *A Taste of the Future*
Mother's Shawls ❀ *Kamal's Illness*

My sisters, Lalit and Kamal, spent nine months of the year in their unheated boarding school, the Himalayan convent in Nainital. They came home only for January, February and March when the mountains turned uncompromisingly frigid. By this time their slender fingers were already red and raw from chilblains. My mother would spend months furiously knitting woollen mittens with openings for the fingers so they could hold their pens and pencils. These, as well as hand-knitted cardigans, socks and mufflers that made their way to the mountain-top school in package after package, hardly helped. My sisters suffered dreadfully from the cold. Of course, they didn't complain. Delhi must have seemed downright balmy to them. I was ecstatic to have my older sisters back for the winter holidays. We celebrated in big ways and small.

On those winter weekends, the men were free by lunchtime on Saturday. We all congregated under the *beri*, our beloved, umbrella-shaped jujube tree that each of us had climbed as children. Weekend lunches were always preceded by beer – for the men. But many of the girls were in their teens now and permitted shandy, a mixture of beer and our carbonated 'lemonade'. Those who wanted to sit in the full sun pulled their chairs away from the *beri's* shade, but most chose to have their heads in the shade and much of their bodies in the sun and so kept adjusting their chairs. It was here that Bhaiyyadada, my very courtly brother, carefully poured me three-quarters of a glass of lemonade and added just enough beer to allow me to feel grown up. The very first sip tasted of a future that lay in waiting.

During this period, we sisters began addressing each other by our initials. I cannot quite pinpoint the exact time or the reasons for it. We probably thought it was 'cool', some sort of Indian cool of the period. I became M, Kamal became K, Lalit was L and Veena was V. When writing, we all spelt the initials differently. I addressed all letters to Lalit 'Dear L' and signed them with an 'M'. Her letters to me began with 'Dear Emm' and were signed 'Ell'. My parents never fell into the game, nor did my eldest brother, but Bhaiyyadada went along and so did our closest cousins and friends. It soon stopped being a game. Our initials *became* our names for each other, names we still use. Today, the group of people that calls me M is a limited club and I guard membership to it jealously. Besides my sisters, my children call me M and so do many of my cousins, nieces, nephews and dear, close friends. Recently in Los Angeles, on the way to a film location, a young actress I hardly knew addressed me as M in a casual sentence, quite out of the blue. I was at first too startled to say anything. But the very next day I had to let her know, as gently as possible, that only those who had known me for at least forty years could address me that way.

(I was reminded then of a story told to me by a young director working for the first time with the legendary and formidable English actress, Dame Edith Evans. Not knowing how to address her, he took the easy way out for the first few days by not addressing her directly at all. Then one day, screwing up his courage, he ventured, 'Edith would you . . .' Dame Edith rose to her full height. 'Edith?' she barked, 'Edith? It will be Edie next.')

Winter was when my mother bought her Kashmiri shawls. Delicate *pashminas* (the real ones, not the imitations available cheaply in the West), fine *shahtooshes* made from the softest mountain goat hair, and *jamevaars*, hand-woven, antique 'paisleys', were all the stuff of dreams, sold only by itinerant *shawl-wallahs* (shawl-sellers) who travelled, generally on recommendation, from house to house. Kashmiri shawls were to Delhi women what furs are, or were, to women in the West. *Pashminas, shahtooshes* and *jamevaars* were the rarer sables and ermines of the trade. They established a woman's credentials as soon as she walked into a room. Unlike some furs, a good Kashmiri shawl could never look cheap or tarty. It always enhanced the wearer, encasing her in solid dignity.

My stylish mother bought a few such shawls each year, adding to her already large collection. Now that her two older daughters were blossoming, she was keeping them in mind too. The *shawl-wallah*, most often a Kashmiri, travelled with an assistant. He carried a small bundle himself and walked in front. The assistant carried a larger bundle and walked behind him. Both were directed to Number 5's back verandah. My mother and older sisters sat down on chairs. They were serious. Veena and I hung about. We, too, would turn into serious shawl-buyers one day. The *shawl-wallah* spread a bedcover on the floor and began opening his bundles.

My mother chose the back verandah because it was possible to be discreet there. After all, our relatives were everywhere. How many shawls we bought and what we paid for them was our business. Besides, she wanted to take full advantage of the southern light. Good light was essential as these *shawl-wallahs*, according to my mother, could not be trusted. Sometimes, she said, they took several old, fraying *jamevaars*, cut off the damaged bits and pieced the good bits together, dyeing sections to make them match. Sometimes a beautiful shawl was riddled with the tiniest moth holes. Only by holding the shawl up to the light would they be visible. Light was needed to check on the fineness of the embroidery, the exact colours and whether there had been any fading.

The *shawl-wallah* would unfold a shawl and hold it up to my mother. My mother would either shake her head and say a firm 'No,' in which case the shawl would be thrown in the direction of the assistant who would refold it and put it away, or my mother would say, 'Put it aside, I will think about it,' in which case the shawl would be put to one side. My canny mother knew that almost as important as the light needed to examine the shawls was the poker face required to fool the *shawl-wallah*. On no account was he to get the slightest hint of which shawl she was really interested in as that would jack up its price.

The shawls were never ticketed with prices. A *shawl-wallah* could ask for whatever the market would bear and that, of course, varied. If, at the end of a day, no shawls had been sold and the *shawl-wallah* needed money, prices could come way down. If the *shawl-wallah* had a hint of the one shawl that was most desired, he could hold off until he got the price he wanted.

Soon there was a heap of 'possible' shawls that my mother might want. She started all over again with this heap. She winnowed them down by making a second selection from the first, again saying 'No' and 'Put it aside.' The heap of 'possibles' got smaller and smaller with each selection until there were only a few left. She asked for their prices and began haggling. She was very good at it. Sometimes she presented the *shawl-wallah* with so many options that he got confused and forgot the ridiculously high prices he had originally quoted. 'If I take this one and this one and this one, how much would it cost?' 'What if I removed this one and added that one?'

Once a *shawl-wallah* came to us with the most stunning green, nineteenth-century *jamevaar*. It was a rare colour and the hand-loomed paisley workmanship was incomparable. It was the only shawl we wanted. Yet my mother went through her usual 'No' and 'Put it aside' for hours until the poor *shawl-wallah* sold it to her for a price she was willing to pay.

March came to an end before I wanted it to, and my sisters went back to their convent school in Nainital. I began to feel lost the second they headed north.

The twin, seemingly contradictory, elements of dependence and resilient independence were being etched into my character. My brothers were absent for much of the first decade of my life. My older sisters were missing for most of my crucial early teens. I used to write to my oldest brother, Brijdada, from Kanpur. He would reply, reassuring me sometimes with letters and sometimes with drawings. Lalit had assumed a semi-motherly role. She was certainly my mentor for all intellectual matters and was the only one who seemed to understand my insecurities enough to try to draw me out of them. Once she and Kamal left for school, I felt bereft.

Since private traumas were never discussed in my family, only smoothed over whenever necessary, these feelings of loss just stayed within me and festered.

At the end of 1946, Lalit graduated from her mountain convent school and returned to Delhi for good. The following year, she was

My father, me (standing to his left), aged about 13, and Veena on holiday in Poona. These were difficult years.

admitted to Indraprastha College, an easy cycling distance from our house.

Around this very time I began to notice my father and mother whispering to each other with worried expressions. Somehow Kamal, who was still in Nainital and everybody's favourite, was involved in this worry. At first I couldn't understand any of it and my parents wouldn't explain. What I did know was that something had happened during sports. Had she fallen down and hurt herself?

*A typical pre-dinner gathering at Number 5. Me, my mother and my aunts.
Kamal sits far left. Number 7 looms in the background.*

There were calls to the school, talk about x-rays, calls to doctors. It seemed that Kamal had noticed swelling and pain in her ankle and had found herself unable to compete in their summer sports day. The nuns had called in doctors who had pronounced it serious. There was talk of a malignant bone tumour in her leg.

Kamal was brought back to Delhi in June of 1947. Doctors poked around doing biopsies and then deep radiation. It was felt that the problem had been brought under control. She would do her final school exams, her Senior Cambridge, from Delhi.

CHAPTER TWENTY-TWO

The Muslim Twins ❋ *Sudha's Vegetarian Delights*
Punjabi Promela ❋ *Our Shared Lunchtime Feasts*
Contacting the Spirit World ❋ *The Icy Hands of Partition*
Mahatma Gandhi ❋ *Spinning for India*
Independence Day and the Bloody Aftermath

There were other changes in the air. World War II was finally over. While Europe and East Asia looked forward to peace, India could anticipate only a wrenching Partition, as it was called, with a fearsome capital P. This Solomon-testing breakup of its being into two entities had already caused mayhem. The British, with Lord Mountbatten as their viceroy in India, were granting India its freedom but not before splitting the country, taking two chunky ribs out of India to form Muslim Pakistan to its east and west. All the secular dreams of nationalists like Jawaharlal Nehru and Mahatma Gandhi that saw Hindus, Muslims, Sikhs and Christians coexisting in a newly independent nation were being crushed into the ground.

The Partition drama was being played out at all levels. The Muslim League, under the guidance of Muhammed Ali Jinnah, had already endorsed the idea of a separate nation for India's Muslims. Nehru and Gandhi were using all means possible *not* to give in to that idea, to keep the country whole. The British were leaving anyway. How much did *they* really care? They were being accused of a history of divide-and-rule tactics that was culminating in Partition. Hindus and Muslims, encouraged by their own fanatics to be ever more mistrustful, were now pitted against one another. Riots were breaking out throughout the country and Gandhi was rushing around trying to quell them with his policy of non-violent resistance.

Until then our school, Queen Mary's, had been a haven of tolerance. Our class was fairly evenly divided between Hindus and Muslims. We picked our friends on the basis of intellectual companionship and common interests, not religion. My intimates included the Muslim twins, Abida and Zahida, Sudha, a vegetarian Jain, and Promela, a Hindu Punjabi.

Abida and Zahida came to school wearing the most exquisite *ghararas* as their lower garments with short *kurtis* (shirts) on top. *Ghararas* were worn only in Muslim families and resembled culottes. However, they were unlike the *izaars* – the wide, floor-length pyjamas – of my mother's childhood. *Ghararas* were so full of gathers that they gave the appearance of being floor-length, ample skirts. As all the gathers were pushed to the back and collected there, the general effect was that of an elegant bustle. Very smart, I thought. I wanted to wear them too. I borrowed a *gharara* from Abida and had our tailor, Ram Narain, copy it several times over. Now all I needed were the long scarves, *chunnis*, the two-and-a-half-yard cloth pieces we draped across our bosoms and then threw back over our shoulders. These were not ordinary *chunnis* but the hand-dyed, hand-pleated ones – often with sparklers in them – that my Muslim friends wore.

I dragged my mother to the market to get a whole bolt of the finest *mulmul* (muslin). I cut this up into two-and-a-half-yard sections and left the pieces in a shop that specialized in covering them with the tiniest embroidered silver stars. Then I rushed them to the dyer and picked the shades I wanted – aqua, a soft, spring-leaf green, maroon, cobalt blue, peach – and left clear instructions that the muslin needed to be heavily starched. Once this was done, I was left to do the hand-pleating myself. Each *chunni* took about two hours if I worked quickly. The highly starched fabric wore my fingers to the bone but I was determined to do it. Abida and Zahida had taught me how.

It needed two people. My mother or my younger sister, Veena, could always be drafted. The second person held a comfortable length of the *chunni* in front of her, as if she were playing the thread game cat's cradle. I sat opposite them with my hands closed in loose fist formation. I grabbed one edge of the fabric between my thumbs and curled fingers and proceeded to form the pleats, one at a time in a kind of horizontal milking action, one hand moving quickly after the other, until I had gone across the whole width. I did this countless times for each *chunni*, then twisted the *chunni* like a rope several times over so the pleats would firm up and hold. I could now float through school just like some of my friends, holding the folds of my *gharara* up elegantly to one side when I ran, my newly dyed, pleated, sparkling *chunni* dangling from my shoulders. I never did manage to look quite as elegant as Abida and Zahida, though. They had single, thick, ever-moving braids going down their backs all the way to the bottom of their hips. My two thinner braids, ending in ridiculous black-ribbon bows, ruined the entire effect.

Abida and Zahida excelled in mathematics and embroidery. I could barely even say the word 'mathematics' without clouds of confusion descending upon me. Mathematics and I were born on two separate planets. When given a choice of higher or lower mathematics in the upper school, I had quickly opted for the lower kind. This allowed me to drop algebra and geometry altogether. Lower mathematics was a startling composite. It consisted of arithmetic, which I could just about manage, and domestic science, a catch-all subject that must have drawn its inspiration directly from *Mrs Beeton's Book of Household Management*. I found myself learning some turn-of-the-century British 'downstairs' refinements, such as how to use a scrubbing board and how to make food for invalids such as blancmange. (I made it and just threw it away, it being totally alien to Indian sensibilities.) I also learnt how to tie a tourniquet and assorted head-to-toe bandages, how to remove stains, basic embroidery stitches and the names and number of bones in the human body. There are two hundred and six bones in the body. You must always remember to count the six in the ears.

In arithmetic, when the very words, 'If it takes a train six hours to travel 145 ...' made me desperate to reach out for a good novel, Abida and Zahida took firm charge of me, guiding me through a labyrinth of ratios and square roots. The genius of these twins, for me at any rate, lay not so much in their mathematical abilities as in their fine embroidery. The school taught us the British standards – embroideries using the cross-stitch, the chain stitch, the herring-bone and others I already knew – but Abida and Zahida could do *kasheeda*. Probably perfected in *purdah* homes where veiled Muslim women were isolated for hours at a time, this was a form of magical embroidery that allowed both sides of a fabric to end up looking exactly the same. There were two right sides and no wrong side. I *had* to learn it, and there were no better teachers than my twin friends.

They also taught me some games. *Gittay* was a pick-up-stones game similar to 'jacks', except we played it with pebbles, and *Pitthoo* was a two-team game, rather like rounders or baseball. *Gittay* and *Pitthoo* were both street games, a world away from the more formal badminton, tennis and cricket I had been raised with. But I loved playing them in my newly donned *gharara* and *chunni* as it allowed me to enter the inner-city life of my peers that I desperately wanted to share.

There was one other way in school of sharing – and actually tasting – the inner city – not the inner city that my mother had introduced me to but the inner city of my growing group of friends. That was at lunch, which we ate together, as far away from the stone school building as possible. We all brought our lunches from home.

The moment the bell clanged for lunchtime play, we would lift our many-tiered tiffin-carriers by their handles and make a dash for the outdoor area at the back of the school. We'd run through the corridor where *burkas* hung on either side in desultory rows, down the back steps, past the ancient neem tree with stone seating built around it and the netball courts. We kept running even beyond the second old neem tree where our Girl Guide classes were held and where our little fingers had been drilled in the art of perfectly executed reef and sheepshank knots. We were aiming for the back of the school grounds where the land sloped upwards and where the heat of the day was kept at bay by the soft breezes wafting under rows of tall, shady trees. Here we stopped, took a few deep breaths, and sat down on the ground to picnic.

Tiffin-carriers were taken apart, tier after tier. What wonders did they contain today? Abida and Zahida could be relied upon to bring meats – and what meats they were! Goat cooked with spinach, browned onions and cardamom or goat with potatoes, cinnamon and cloves. It was not so much the ingredients as they were not all that different from the ones we used at home, though we did use less chilli powder. What made these dishes special was the hand that put these ingredients together and the order and timing it chose to use. That hand had a different rhythm, a different energy to my mother's and to our own Hindu cooks from Himalayan villages. It produced a Muslim result.

That was the peculiarity of India's cuisines. There were dozens of traits, habits and traditions that could be used to define regional foods. But such definitions were never entirely satisfactory as there also hovered over each dish an air of indefinable religious sensibility that could be seen and tasted but eluded pinpointing. This stamp was present even if the dishes had the same names but were prepared by families of differing religions, even though these families might have lived in the same city for centuries.

Abida and Zahida's food was inner-city, Delhi and Muslim. As my fingers tore off a small piece of meat from a bone, formed a morsel with the *roti* (flat, whole-wheat bread), dipped the morsel in the spicy meat sauce (*shorva*) and then placed it in my mouth, I could taste all three influences. In the winter, when fat from the meat dish formed a stiff yellowish-red icing over its surface, the twins heated up that particular container of the tiffin-carrier over a small paraffin stove, which they lit with a match. Those smells – the cardamom, cinnamon, the paraffin and the freshly lit match – would swirl around my head as I sat through the next class, whatever it was.

Sudha was also a Delhi girl. Her family, like mine, had moved out of the Old City and had chosen to live in Lutyens's New Delhi, on Ferozshah Road, named after the same emperor whose ruined battlements provided the foundation stones of my great-great-grandfather's inner-city home. Sudha's food was as Jain as Abida's and Zahida's was Muslim. Completely vegetarian, it was devoid of onion and garlic as those bulbs were thought to arouse base passions; it contained no tomatoes or beets as their colour was reminiscent of blood; and featured no real root vegetables (though rhizomes were acceptable) as pulling out roots killed the entire plant. The preservation of life demanded by her religion didn't stop her food being scrumptious in a haughty, austere way. Nor did it prevent her sharing her food – green beans, peas, chickpea flour dumplings or cauliflower – with us.

Promela's family were relaxed Delhi Punjabis. A few 'modern' Punjabis had begun giving their children semi-Western names, hoping to propel them fully into a modern world they were only half in at the time. Their food, though, would never change. They did not want it to change. It would always stay Indian, Punjabi-Indian at that. They were proud of it.

Promela lived within the inner-city walls in Daryagunj, an area that was once by the Yamuna before the river idiosyncratically moved further east. It was less crowded there than in the heart of the inner city. Here roads and houses had at least some room to breathe. She too lived in a joint family, in a house as large as Number 7 but without the countrified gardens. We visited each other often.

She brought *parathas* (griddle breads) stuffed with cauliflower, and mango pickle to eat with it. In the winter, Promela's tiffin-carrier was crammed with *makki ki roti* (corn flat breads) and *sarson ka saag* (mustard greens), all so buttery-rich and mouth-wateringly good that she knew we would devour every last bit.

I always found my own food the least interesting and barely touched it. It was all too familiar. The others might enjoy my *poori* (fried bread) and *aloo* (potatoes with ginger), but I wanted the contents of *their* tiffin-carriers. After we ate, sharing what we could, we either played *gittay* or wrote the letters of the alphabet in a circle on the dry earth or on the floor of the art room verandah, making an instant Ouija board and, using an ink-bottle top as a guide, called the spirits. We were big into spirits then, into life, death, love, even elopement. Shahida, one of the Muslim girls in my class with pale-green eyes, was crazily in love with a first cousin and was contemplating running away. We were following that story closely.

The school, we had been told, was built on an old graveyard. Spirits seemed to be there for the asking. We pestered the spirits with questions about exams, about our crushes and loves and about our futures. Most of the answers were spelled out without hesitation but sometimes the ink-bottle top refused to be contained within the Ouija circle. It rose upwards by itself and flew out angrily, landing yards away. We didn't know whether to be alarmed or to giggle.

Most of our teenage friendships withered and died as soon as talk of Partition began. It was as if two icy hands had descended and split our class into two: Muslims on one side, fully armed with appropriate arguments, demanding a partition of the country; Hindus on the other, with their own much-repeated counter-arguments, saying 'Never'. Not surprisingly, I was left in the middle, trying to hold the two sides together. Not surprisingly, I was mistrusted by both sides. I didn't belong to one and I seemed to be a traitor to the other. The hurts and angers were such that we turned into a class of righteous fanatics. I would not, could not, allow all Muslims to be condemned as some of my Hindu friends wanted but I also could not bear to see India divided and, as I saw it, a great country frittered away in bits and pieces. Tolerance and nuanced thinking had been shoved out of the window. It was an unbearable time of hard-headed black and white, them and us.

Without giving it much thought, at that somewhat tender age I had become a firm follower of Mahatma Gandhi, with my dear, soft-hearted father and mother serving as my guides. I had initially become agitated with their descriptions of the Salt March. This was not in our school history books and predated my birth, but I already knew all the details of Gandhi's Dandi Salt March on 12 March 1930. At that time our British colonial rulers had decided to impose a draconian law that prohibited salt production by anyone they did not control. This law affected every single Indian. We all ate salt and this felt like a salt tax. Gandhi decided not only to make his own salt in a seaside town named Dandi but to stage a very public 240-mile march to get there.

In my earlier years, Gandhi had begun advocating that we stop our reliance on foreign fabrics and that we spin, weave and produce our own handloom cloth as a symbol of our independence struggle. By now, I was determined to participate and bought myself a spinner. At least I would spin the cotton thread. The simple spinning gadgetry, sold to millions of eager Indians, was housed in a black box, similar in shape to the portable, wind-up gramophone I also possessed. Instead of a spinning wheel it held a simpler spinning turntable that I could rotate with my left hand while my right hand expertly pulled a ball of cotton wool into a fine thread. Every week I delivered several large spools of freshly spun thread to a central collection centre.

As anticipated, the British soon drew final lines through the India they were partitioning. Produced in some faraway office, the newly-formed boundaries cut right through the middle of farms, villages, rivers and homes. A wail went up from the nation. Fear and uncertainty ruled. Would the new Muslim Pakistan allow Hindus to coexist? How would a Muslim minority really fare in the new secular India?

Independence Day for India was 15 August 1947, two days after my fourteenth birthday. My father took me to watch the transfer of power at India Gate where a statue of Queen Victoria stood guard right in the centre of a wide Lutyens boulevard called Kingsway at that time. I cannot remember where we parked our car but it must have been at quite a distance. We walked and walked through dense crowds – hundreds of thousands of us had collected there – and stood near enough to Kingsway to have a clear view of Jawaharlal Nehru and Lord Mountbatten riding down in an open horse carriage, both exceedingly handsome in all white. The Union Jack was formally lowered and the Indian tricolour went up. We screamed our lungs out. Thousands of caps were flung skyward. I felt giddy.

The joy did not last too long. In what was the new West Pakistan, Muslim fanatics began butchering Hindus and Sikhs and appropriating their houses. Hindus in the truncated India began slaughtering Muslims, whom they blamed for the break-up of their country. Neighbours who had trusted each other now betrayed each other. Some neighbours who had never paid much attention to each other now hid and saved each other. Mobs marched through villages, towns and cities, killing those of faiths other than their own. Cornered men would be asked to drop their pants to distinguish circumcised Muslims from uncircumcised Hindus. If what came into view did not suit the viewers, daggers, guns and knives put a quick end to precious lives.

A massive, multidirectional migration began: Hindus crammed trains heading for India, clinging to doors and roofs; Muslims jammed trains heading for the two Pakistans. Sometimes the trains arrived at their destinations filled with nothing but dead bodies, having been intercepted by a mob with massacre on its mind. A million people died. Several million lost all their belongings as they ran or were chased from their homes. Angry, hapless refugees were piling up on both sides of the new borders.

Until then, I had seen the men in my family pick up guns only to hunt for venison, partridge, duck and quail. But there was fear in our houses too. Unruly gangs – some bent on religious mischief, some just old-fashioned looters taking advantage of the chaos – were on the attack. This time family guns were being picked up and patrols organized to protect our neighbourhood. I would hear my father say, 'You two take the two a.m. shift. Patrol from Number 5 to Number 8 on Jumna Road and walk back on Raj Narain Road the Number 4 way.' All the men – our fathers, brothers, uncles and cousins – oiled and polished their guns with no sense of adventure or enjoyment. One night the mob got so close we could hear the wild cries and shouts. We barricaded ourselves indoors, fearing for our men still patrolling the streets. But the mob melted away before doing us any harm.

This was not the case with the mob advancing on the house of Dr Joshi, Shibbudada's close friend and uncle to one of Lalit's dearest friends. As it marched menacingly through the gate, Dr Joshi thought he could reason with the leaders and approached them in friendship. They shot him dead. When Shibbudada received the call, he jumped into his two-tone Chevy. We begged him not to go as he would be driving through dangerous sections of the Old City but he paid no heed. I remember so well seeing the back of his car as it sped out of the Number 7 gate and fearing that he too would be shot and we would never see him again.

The Old City had erupted. Hindus and Muslims, who had lived

there cheek by jowl for centuries, were now turning on each other. Mainji's son, my inner-city first cousin, was in his late teens at the time. He left his house for some minor shopping and did not return for several days. By then he had lost his mind. Was he beaten, raped, tortured? He never spoke coherently after that.

Delhi's Muslims began disappearing, making their way to Pakistan. All of my Muslim classmates left without farewells. I can only assume they had safe journeys. I have not seen even one of them since. Amina's father, rightly gauging the roughness of the Novelty Cinema area and Delhi's general instability, bundled up his family and deposited it in London. He, however, chose to stay in India, rising much later to be Mayor of Delhi. My father's dearest friends, Bashir Zaidi and Zakir Hussain, also chose to stay. One would become Vice-Chancellor of Aligarh University and a Member of Parliament and the other the President of India. But other Muslim friends of his did leave. Badr-ul-Islam had a large, grand house on Curzon Road (now Kasturba Gandhi Marg) in Lutyens's New Delhi. His sons were friends of my brothers, often going on hunts together or playing bridge at each other's homes. They all left for Karachi. One of the sons would marry into the politically powerful Bhutto family of Pakistan. Once they had moved out, a family of desperate Punjabi refugees – the Bhagats from Lahore – moved in, not into Badr-ul-Islam's mansion but into the servants' quarters over the garage at the back. By the oddest coincidence, we would get to know this family with its several young daughters as well. One of the daughters would become my sister Kamal's best friend, and her older sister, the personal secretary to Prime Minister Indira Gandhi.

Shibbudada did return safely from Dr Joshi's home only to report that most of the city had turned into a hell. That didn't stop him from riding out in his Chevy again and again to escort his Muslim musician friends from the inner city to planes and trains headed for Pakistan. Many, like the *sarangi* maestro, Bundu Khan, left India with the greatest reluctance after much urging from his family.

Delhi, as we knew it, ceased to exist. Its vibrant Hindu-Muslim culture, its nuanced rules of etiquette, its unfailing politeness and its unique sense of hospitality began to fade away. Urdu, the language it had given birth to, went into a fatal decline. Depleted of many of its original inhabitants, and in a spirit of 'the king is dead, long live the king', Delhi began filling up with new citizens, refugees from the Punjab.

No refugee centre could contain them all. They poured in by the thousands. Once a modest-sized ancient city of little over a million people, Delhi was to bustle with more than thirteen million. The refugees took over all open spaces to set up little shops, markets and shanties, anything to help them survive. The city began expanding haphazardly in all directions without any of Lutyens's innate sophistication or the Moghul's guiding principles of symmetry and grandeur.

On 30 January 1948, Mahatma Gandhi was shot and killed.

A few days earlier my mother had asked me if I wanted to attend one of Gandhiji's prayer meetings (we called Gandhi 'Gandhiji', out of respect), as she was planning to do so. These meetings were held with some regularity at the grand residence of one of India's richest industrialists, Birla. One edge of the landscaped garden was at a height and looked down, after a sheer drop, upon a large open field, forming a natural stage and auditorium. Gandhi came to this stage in the early evenings to pray and talk.

The prayer meetings were non-sectarian and non-denominational. Gandhi believed not in one nation under God but a world, a universe under God – under the same God, whatever different name people chose to address Him by. He embraced India's Untouchables and included all faiths in his hymns. His lectures were about tolerance and man's common humanity.

Of course I wanted to go, I told my mother.

We set off in the late afternoon. The driver had warned us that huge crowds attended these meetings and traffic would be slow. It was worse than slow. Delhi dust mixed with January's *uppala* smoke swirled around thousands of unbudging cars that honked and beeped as if that would somehow facilitate a forward movement. All order had broken down. Instead of one neat lane, cars had angled themselves to the left and right, hoping to escape to a magical, fast-moving path. There was no going forwards or backwards. I feared that Gandhi's prayer meeting would come to a close before we could reach the field.

But we inched forward and got there. There was a sea of people. We joined them, taking our place cross-legged on the ground, just like everybody else. Gandhi came in a white *dhoti* (loin cloth) and shawl, escorted by two young women. We looked up at the stage. He folded his hands, bowed, and the hymns, sung by his followers on stage, began:

> *Ishwar Allah taray naam*
> *Sub ko sanmati dey bhagwan . . .*
> (Ishwar, the Hindu name for God, and Allah,
> the Muslim one, are but names for You,
> Oh God, grant us some wisdom/tolerance)

We all knew the hymns and sang along. When Gandhi himself spoke, it was in a toothless whisper, amplified as best as possible by a microphone. We listened raptly. The sea of people – taxi drivers, farmers, carpenters, sweepers, film tycoons and business moguls – were silent.

Just a few days later Gandhi was shot three times. He was on his way to a prayer meeting with his usual escorts, walking towards the same stage at Birla House where I had so recently seen him, when the shots rang out. He sighed, '*Hey Ram*' ('O God') and died. We heard of it on the radio. The whole city heard of it. Our family was in Number 5. We rushed out on to the street, as if an earthquake had struck. All our relatives were on the street too. Numbers 7, 16, 14, 12 and 10 had spilled out all their inhabitants for an impromptu wake. We cried, sharing our shock and disbelief. Our fear too. At that time, we didn't know who had done the shooting. If it were to turn out to be a Muslim, more killings and riots would surely follow.

That night our first Prime Minister, Jawaharlal Nehru, spoke to the nation on the radio: 'The light has gone out of our lives and there is darkness now ...' his voice rising and falling in the soft, warm cadence that only he possessed.

The assassin was a member of an ultra-orthodox Hindu party that demanded a Hindu India, not the secular, tolerant country of Gandhi and Nehru's dreams. In our family, there was some indefinable sense of relief but great anger as well at any version of religious certainty that could lead to such a senseless murder.

We were all present at Kingsway to view Gandhi's funeral procession, standing at the same spot where, just a few months earlier, my father and I had seen our new national flag unfurled. We wanted to attend the cremation at Rajghat by the river but the crowds were so thick we got just close enough to watch the white smoke from his funeral pyre dance upwards to meet the clouds.

CHAPTER TWENTY-THREE

Punjabi Influences ❀ Food with New Attitude
Bazaar and Tandoori Foods ❀ A Taste of Spam
Sunday Lunchtimes

Refugees from the Punjab settling in Delhi had brought with them their own language, Punjabi, their unique entrepreneurial spirit boosted by a hearty physical energy, and their own culture. Delhi succumbed and became, to a large extent, a Punjabi town. The martial Sikhs, who were once Punjab's fearsome horsemen, monopolized another kind of vehicle, becoming the movers and shakers of the newly created Delhi taxi service. Because it was the capital city and housed a central government that drew civil servants from around the country, Delhi began to develop a national consciousness. As new embassies slowly established themselves, Delhi picked up the heady air of international sophistication as well.

There was a major change, a revolution really, in the city's food. Before independence, most upper-class and middle-class families ate at home. Amongst Hindu families like ours, cleanliness was certainly next to Godliness. We bathed at least once a day in the winter and at least twice daily in the summer, always in flowing water. Bathtubs were anathema. 'How can those people sit in dirty water!' my mother would exclaim, gesturing her head in the general direction of the West.

We ate only home-cooked food and washed our hands and mouths before and after meals. Eating out was not condoned. As my father said repeatedly, 'Who knows what germs lurk about in *outside* food. Perhaps a dirty finger has been poked into a bowl or perhaps clean food has been removed with a *jhoota* [previously used] spoon.'

Jhoota was a big word in our home. If someone's mouth had touched a food, it was taboo to anyone else. It was now considered *jhoota*, or tainted by the mouth. I never shared a whole apple, pear or peach with anyone, not even my sisters. Once one of us had taken a bite, it was definitely *jhoota* and unavailable to all others, even if the person who started on the fruit could not finish it. My mother then just said, 'Oh, how could you waste it like that,' and threw it away. If one person drank from a glass of water, soft drink or whisky, it was theirs. No-one else could take a sip. Not a soul in our family was ever heard to suggest, 'Taste mine. Take a sip of mine.' (Even today, if a friend in America or England says innocently, 'Taste my Bloody Mary. It's wonderful. It has something unusual in it. Tell me what it is,' I am at first paralysed into a Hamlet-like state of inaction. I then fall on my sword and taste it as every atom of my body yells, 'No, no, noooo.') As children we played dirty rotten games with each other by quickly licking the fruit, chocolate or sandwich we had our eye on and then singing wickedly, 'Its *jhoota* now. You can't have it.'

A few strange contradictions did, however, manage to work their way into the fabric of our pure, clean lives. They took the form of special bazaar foods. There were the aforementioned *parathas* our mother let us eat on the quiet – these definitely slipped under the radar – but there were others that were officially sanctioned. The first of these was the *aloo bedvi* (sauced potatoes and stuffed *pooris*) we got on the odd weekend from Ghantayvala Halvai for breakfast.

This *halvai*, or sweet-maker, who had his shop in the very centre of Chandni Chowk, the main street of Moghul Delhi, specialized in sweets and savoury snacks. It was the savoury snacks I was interested in. Most weekends in Number 5, we had eggs for breakfasts, with ham, bacon or sausages from the English shop, Spencers, in Kashmiri Gate. But every now and then my mother prevailed and my father let the driver go out to procure a breakfast of her choice from the Old City, the very Hindu *aloo bedvi*. My father justified this indulgence by saying, 'At least the food is cooked and hot and therefore free of germs. Besides, we serve it on our own clean plates that have not been washed in filthy bazaar water.'

My father's own choice of bazaar foods – and he certainly had his indulgences – were far more questionable, especially in light of his own articulated standards. He, and my brothers for that matter, all loved Muslim foods from another inner-city bazaar area, the one that surrounded the seventeenth-century mosque, Jama Masjid. They liked the kebabs, especially the satiny, crumbling-at-the-touch, tubular *seekh kebabs* made by wrapping very finely ground, perfectly seasoned meat around thick skewers and grilling them on charcoal braziers. They also enjoyed the hamburger-like *shami kebabs*, made by boiling minced meat with spices, making a pâté-like paste with the mixture, forming patties and browning them. But *shami kebabs* could be made at home. Our family excelled at them. What we didn't do was the grilling that *seekh kebab* demanded or the baking that the accompanying Muslim breads required.

Over the centuries, Kayastha families like ours had acquired the dubious reputation of being *sharabi-kebabis*, lovers of alcohol and kebabs. This applied only to the men as the women almost never drank. They imbibed only 'soft drinks'. Although my mother spoke no English she did know how to say 'soft drink', two words required frequently in company. Even though they didn't partake of the alcohol, many of the women had taken to relishing their meats. One rather large, exquisitely beautiful, green-eyed cousin of mine was asked if she cared for sweets, to which she replied langorously, 'Nooo, not really. If I have any room left in my stomach at all, I just eat another *kofta* [meatball].'

Whenever we had a big party – and sometimes it was just a large family gathering – the men demanded that their much-loved kebabs and Muslim breads be sent for. A driver was dispatched but not before he was given clean platters, tablecloths, napkins and tea towels so that when the food reached us it upheld the family's standards of cleanliness, at least outwardly.

The driver made sure that the breads, the *roomali rotis* (handkerchief breads) – breads as thin, soft, fine and large as a man's handkerchief – and the *bakarhkani* – dense, thick, multi-layered, buttery flat breads – were wrapped in the tablecloths. He handed our clean platters to the Jama Masjid kebab-maker and supervised as the *seekh kebabs* were arranged in neat rows and paper-thin red onion rings spread generously over the top. The onion rings were not only a much-loved accompaniment but also helped keep the kebabs moist. The onion rings were raw – my father supposedly mistrusted raw bazaar food – and they had been soaked in water – filthy bazaar water? – to erase some of their sharpness. Yet the finicky men in our family devoured them without a care.

Until then, that was the extent of the 'outside' food we ate, other than the odd pastries and cakes we bought from Davicos and Wengers, English teahouses, or the semi-Western meals we ate at our parents' clubs. Then a restaurant called Moti Mahal opened on a main road in Daryagunj on the edge of the Old City. More a set of rough and ready stalls than a real restaurant, it had a set of large clay ovens shaped like vats embedded in its floor. These were known as *tandoors*. Delhi was entranced. It had never seen the likes of them before nor eaten the tandoori foods these ovens produced.

Young, whole, roasted chickens emerged so tender and moist they could be pulled apart and devoured in seconds. Light, bubbly *naan* breads, made by slapping elongated tear-drop shapes against the heated tandoor walls, were pulled out with long hooks. These could be torn and wrapped around the meat. *Kali dal* (whole black beans) provided the accompaniment, cooked overnight in an earthen vessel, partially buried in the *tandoor*'s fading embers. The only condiment offered at the table was a bowl of small, whole pickled onions. This was food with a new attitude. Its very simplicity and freshness was modern and enticing. There was nothing like it in Delhi. Moti Mahal was packing them in.

This was Punjabi food from what had once been India's north-west frontier, near its border with Afghanistan. When India was partitioned, fleeing Hindu refugees from the newly formed West Pakistan gathered their valuables and ran in an easterly direction. They carried their *tandoors* with them so they could cook along the way. One such family that fled all the way to Delhi decided to open Moti Mahal and offer its plain village cooking to a city of culinary sophisticates. The rest, as they say, is history.

Tandoori food – good, bad and mostly indifferent – has been produced by almost every major Indian restaurant since then. The trend started first in Delhi and then spread throughout the globe. In Delhi, other Punjabi entrepreneurs noted Moti Mahal's success and felt they could do better by serving *tandoori* food on starched table-cloths. They would add Moghul delicacies, even Western hors d'oeuvres of baked beans and sardines, to the menu and have a fancy bar that served all manner of alcoholic drinks, including hard cider. They would also offer the occasional weekend dinner dance. Gaylord in New Delhi was one such place. It too was very successful. The new independent Delhi was in an extroverted, celebratory mood, and restaurants became the place to express this new freedom. The conservative, mild-mannered, softly spoken Delhiwallahs were soon following the more outgoing Punjabis and eating publicly. New restaurants, coffee shops and *dhabas* were opening daily.

The *dhaba* was entirely of Punjabi origin. Once a simple roadside café for lorry drivers on the road, or any passers-by, it turned into a fixture in the small shacks and stalls of Delhi's newer markets set up by refugees. It served Punjabi staples such as *chana-bhatura* (spicy chickpeas with deep-fried leavened breads), as well as quick stir-fries made in the *karhai* (Indian cast-iron wok) with *paneer* (very freshly made cheese) and tomatoes.

Punjabis, like Texans, did everything bigger and better. If the entire nation had a passion for dairy products, the Punjabis indulged in them even more. They preferred rich milk with cream floating on the top and drank it in large amounts. When they made yoghurt, they used water buffalo milk with its higher percentage of fat, often reducing it over low heat until it had the texture of cream. This they set into the richest – and tastiest – yoghurt you could ever hope to eat. If they made *lassi* (a yoghurt drink) with this, they added some cold milk for extra richness and then served it in tall glasses, each with the capacity of an average blender. (I use the few Punjabi *lassi* glasses I own as vases for long-stemmed flowers.) They not only used *ghee* (clarified butter) for all their cooking, frowning on oils, but smeared the most generous dollops of homemade white butter on their *rotis* (flat breads) and greens. One of my twin cousins married a Punjabi who impressed me greatly by telling me that, as a child, he was given a spoonful of *ghee* in the morning to make him big and strong. *Paneer* (fresh cheese) dishes were also Punjabi specialities: *mattar paneer* (*paneer* with peas), *saag paneer* (*paneer* with spinach) and *paneer bhurji* (shredded *paneer* stir-fried with onions, ginger, green chillies, green coriander and tomatoes). The first two of these would become a firm part of the Indian restaurant repertoire, in Delhi to begin with and then around the world.

Most grocers now carried big wheels of *paneer*, made by curdling milk with the previous day's whey, collecting the curds in a cheese-cloth and pressing down briefly on the bundle. Anyone could buy a chunk of the fresh cheese, along with the peas, onions and ginger they needed.

Although World War II was over, we were belatedly being bombarded with its leftovers in the form of mysterious boxes known as K-Rations (the US military meal packets). Delhi was awash with them. It was almost as if the rectangular, brownish-khaki boxes had been dug up from some forgotten hoard and then floated down to us on a million parachutes. This may have actually happened as we were also awash with parachute 'silk', which was being transformed quickly into blouses, skirts, sarees and curtains by Delhi's masses.

I never thought then of checking the expiry date on the K-Rations. All I remember is that my cousins and I tore them open as if they were Christmas presents, pulling out each carefully fitted tin or package with the greatest glee. Thus I was introduced to my first olive, my first fruit cocktail and my first taste of Spam. I rolled mouthfuls slowly around my tongue and pronounced each of them to be exotic and wonderful. I had never eaten tinned fruit or meat before.

While we, the younger generation, now routinely picked up tandoori foods from Moti Mahal for our picnics, stopped now and then at a *dhaba* for a snack of *chana-bhatura* and regularly patronized restaurants like Gaylord, our meals at home, controlled by the adults, stayed steadfastly the same. No Punjabi influence filtered in. K-Rations stayed out of the dining room and were dismissed as children's rubbish.

All our meals were in Number 5, and our little kitchen there was humming busily from morning until night. Sunday lunches provided us with two of our most beloved dishes, one with a Hindu pedigree, the other with a Muslim one. My mother and I preferred the local Hindu *karhi-chawal* by a few degrees. Made with chickpea flour and buttermilk, it was soupy and sour, filled with light, bobbing dumplings and served with rice. The men preferred the very Muslim *pullao* (pilaf) – by a few degrees. So we alternated between the two unevenly, somehow always in favour of the men.

By mid-morning the aroma of boiling basmati rice would spread through the house. I found myself drawn to the kitchen to watch my mother make the dumplings. She would put the chickpea flour in a bowl and slowly add water, mixing away until she had a thick, smooth paste. She would beat the paste with her little hand, my father's signet ring firmly on, until it fluffed up and turned quite pale. 'This is the step that makes the *pakoris* (dumplings) light and fluffy,' she explained. She carried the bowl to our simple, hand-built, brick-and-earth stove, lit with charcoal. A *karhai* (wok) with hot oil already sat on a burner. My mother picked up a lump of paste with her fingers and released it with her thumb. It plopped into the oil, sank and then quickly rose to the surface, creating a frenzy of little noisy bubbles. She dropped another dumpling and another until the surface of the oil was covered with them, all bubbling away. When they were golden and cooked through, she scooped them up with a slotted spoon and released them into the hot, soupy *karhi* to soak and soften. Her dumplings, the heart of a good Delhi *karhi*, were always perfect.

Pullao Sundays were another matter. They were, without a doubt, a product of our Muslim heritage. The proper name for our *pullao* would probably be *yakhni pullao*, *yakhni* being the flavoured stock used for cooking the rice. (Even the name of the dish was derived from Arabic and Persian sources.) That flavour was heady. Pieces of goat, from the neck and ribs in particular, were boiled with whole spices – cardamom, cumin, cinnamon, cloves, bay leaves, fennel seeds, black peppercorns and coriander seeds as well as a whole onion and chunks of ginger. The stock simmered slowly. We would inhale aromas of the feast-to-be as it cooked for hours, getting hungrier by the minute. Once the meat was tender, it was removed and the soup strained to produce the precious *yakhni*. The rest was easy. All that was needed was to brown the meat with sliced onions and some black cardamom pods, add basmati rice and *yakhni*, and allow the rice to steam through. A *yakhni pullao* was earthy, basic and honest. Rather like a good pasta or risotto dish, it required only choice ingredients and perfect timing.

Pullao days were good because my mother indulged my father completely. She added on the *koftas* (meatballs) he so loved, some gingery green beans, a potato *raita* made with yoghurt that had just the right degree of sourness he was partial to, and a spicy salad made with tomatoes, onions and cucumbers. The table was always graced with spring onions stuck, green-side up, in a Waterford crystal glass filled with water. They did double duty, serving as our floral – green, at any rate – centrepiece as well. We chased each mouthful of *pullao* with a bite of the spring onion, and then went on to the *koftas* and green beans. After such a meal, bodies naturally turned lethargic so *pullao* Sunday lunches were invariably followed by serious *pullao* Sunday naps.

CHAPTER TWENTY-FOUR

The Looming Banyan Tree ❋ *New School Friends and Fresh
Tastes* ❋ *Learning to Love Hindi* ❋ *Two Types of Indian
Hated Cookery Lessons* ❋ *Divine Potatoes*

Until I was well into my teens, my father's two-toned, beige and chocolate Plymouth had dropped me off at school. I now insisted that I was old enough to travel by myself on a bicycle. I had a basket in front for my books, and my three-tiered tiffin-carrier dangling from the handlebars. Extra tennis shoes or clothing required for school plays or sports could be clipped to the saddle.

My father had taught me how to ride a bicycle on our back lawn in Kanpur. Holding the small-sized lady's bicycle from the back, he had pushed me around the badminton court, along the rose beds and up near the back wall until one day he just gave a big shove and let go. I was cycling by myself and didn't even know it, peddling hard and fast, the little wheels turning like a dynamo.

That was how I cycled throughout my childhood years in India, afraid that if I slowed down I would lose control and fall. I had a million fears, the first being the looming banyan tree that stood twenty cycling-seconds away from our house. It was an ancient specimen with the dimensions of a cathedral, its many branches drooping to the earth and re-rooting themselves again and again to form hundreds of crazy Gaudí-like arches. It was home to so many creatures that passing under it presented a world of hazards. Bird droppings were one of the more palpable ones. If I did not hit the pedals, I could receive a virtual shower.

Less palpable was a presence that lingered there imperceptibly, one I had been introduced to by our *aayaas*, the nannies who cared for us. Each successive *aayaa* – whether Hindu or Christian, whether illiterate or semi-literate – had a similar stash of stories set in a pantheistic world filled with ghosts, spirits, giants and fairies. We loved hearing their tales and, quite wisely, refrained from repeating them to our parents lest this source be silenced. We quietly added the heroes and demons of these tales to our own growing lists drawn from Greek and Hindu mythology, from the Bible, from comics, films and from the books we read daily. One of the *aayaas* impressed on me again and again that I should beware the spirits that peopled banyan trees. Then she told me a 'true' story that would haunt me for the rest of my life.

There was a young man, she said, who had to pass under a banyan tree every morning as he travelled to work. A female spirit who lived in the tree watched the young man on his daily journey and fell deeply in love with him. She begged the leader of the spirits to let her assume a human form so she could meet the young man. The leader at first refused but finally relented, saying, 'I will grant you a human form for only as long as you live a proper human life, performing only human actions. The moment you do anything extraordinary and spirit-like, this boon will end.'

The spirit was transformed into a beautiful damsel who appeared before the young man repeatedly in different settings until he fell in love with her and married her. They had a joyous life together, eventually producing a son. She lived as a human, cooking, cleaning and caring for her son in a small second-floor apartment. On weekdays, the husband went to work and the boy, eventually, to school.

One day, when the husband was still at work, the boy – who was about ten now – asked his mother if he could go downstairs to play in the common garden. The mother gave her permission but sat at the upstairs window, watching. She noticed that the local young bully had picked up a large boulder and was approaching her son from the back. She watched as the bully raised the boulder to smash it down on her son's head. Without thinking, she stretched out her arm – and stretched it and stretched it – until she was able to reach the bully and push him aside. Then, of course, she had to disappear and become, once again, a spirit in the banyan tree.

The road, as it passed under the vast edifice of the banyan tree, was on a slight incline. I lowered my head and, with my heart throbbing and two neatly beribboned pigtails flying behind me, raced uphill at top speed. No birds or long-armed spirits were going to get me.

From there onwards, I travelled mostly on back roads, choosing to enter the school through its front gate on a quiet, narrow lane and not the back gate, which was on an unsavoury busy thoroughfare. Sometimes I was followed by lecherous *goondas* (petty hoodlums) in loose pyjamas and fitted shirts who came too close and whispered things good little girls were not supposed to hear, but I looked straight ahead and cycled away.

The school was still reeling from the upheavals of independence and Partition. Perhaps to provide an overlay of order, it had been decided that all the schoolgirls would wear uniforms. The uniforms would not be the traditional navy blues or browns of most schools. Ours were to be mauve. Not a nice mauve but a vile one that even Mother Nature might not tolerate. Our *kameezes* (long shirts) and *chunnis* (long scarves) would be mauve while our *salwars* (baggy pants) would be white.

There were hardly any Muslims left, none at all in my class. Newer girls had poured in and we were just getting to know them. Manoranjana, a refugee, was a tall Sikh who had fled a small town in the Punjab. Hindi was not her language at all so our school had made an exception and given her permission to study Punjabi with a private teacher who came for her alone. English was not her language either though she spoke it well enough. She sighed frequently in the English classes. She hadn't grown up with any of the books we had absorbed since childhood – from English nursery rhymes to Dickens – or the everyday proverbs we used, and felt like an alien. But, like Abida and Zahida, she was brilliant at mathematics. With this subject, which was a language of its own, all her awkwardness vanished and she became serene and confident.

My Hindi, meanwhile, had improved by leaps and bounds, and all because of a new teacher. He was tall, slightly pock-marked and bespectacled, the only male among our teaching staff. I was shocked that Queen Mary's had hired him at all. At first, our relationship was somewhat distant and wary. I was, on the surface, this bold, Westernized know-it-all; he, in his Indian *kurta* and *pyjamas*, was shy, hesitant and seemingly ultra-conservative. When I was asked to read in class from a book we were studying, I watched his eyes glaze over at the slowness of my attempt. Reading Hindi was still an effort for me. I couldn't just zip along. Whether I was doing the reading or listening to someone else, I couldn't let a sentence pass by without making sure I knew the meaning of every word in it. With my Hindi vocabulary still deficient, I was the cause of many stoppages. He frowned at me repeatedly for slowing down his class.

His attitude towards me changed entirely after a homework assignment. It was the kind of assignment usually set by English teachers: write an essay about your holidays … write about someone you admire … write about the happiest day in your life. Most of the children hated such subjects as they seemed too vague and general. I, perversely, loved them as I felt I was being granted the freedom to write whatever I wanted, create a holiday I hadn't had, conjure up a 'person to admire' who didn't exist or turn what had been a tedious day into a 'happy' one.

Until then our Hindi teachers had stuck to questions raised in our textbooks. This new teacher, Masterji as we called him, asked us to write an essay on our relatives.

Here was a subject I could handle or at least manipulate to my own design. What was becoming clearer to me as I was getting older was that there were two distinct types of Indians. There was my kind of Indian, a privileged product of British colonial India who spoke English fluently but also spoke Hindi. We ate at a table with napkins, knives and forks, but would eat with our hands when we wished. We were avid cinema-goers who watched both Western and Indian films, and we could talk about Tudor England just as easily as about Moghul India. One part of us was completely Indian but there was this sophisticated Western overlay, a familiarity and ease with the West that set us apart.

If my father had decided to send us to Mahila Vidyalay, the Hindi-language school in Kanpur, we might have become the second kind of Indian. Most of India consisted of this kind of Indian whose mastery of English was nil or limited, who – like my mother and her relatives in the Old City, like Manoranjana and, yes, like Masterji, my Hindi teacher – lived much more traditional, unbifurcated lives. Were they the real Indians and we just hybrids created by a particular time and place? Would we now, after independence, just be ploughed under or left with no standing in our new society?

I didn't really want to write about my relatives. I wanted to write about the relationship between the two different types of Indians and to pass it off as an essay on 'my relatives'. I devised a short story about a poorer, more traditional man (someone, say, like Masterji) coming for dinner to the home of his richer, more Westernized relatives (to a family, say, like ours). I decided I would view this encounter through the eyes of the two youngest children of the Westernized family. In this way I could comment and analyse, be rueful, compassionate or rude, whatever I wished. I didn't need to dig up big, Sanskritized Hindi words. After all, the story was being told from the point of view of children. My own vocabulary would be sufficient.

I wrote the story and added my book to the pile of homework exercise books on Masterji's desk. The following week we got our homework back. Masterji handed out one book at a time, making small comments as he did so: 'Good effort,' 'Watch your spelling,' and the like. My book was last. He slapped it on his table, took off his glasses and just looked at me as if seeing me for the first time. 'Brilliant,' he said, 'that was just brilliant.' He handed me back the book, still staring at me. I opened it up just a little bit to peek at my marks. I had received ten out of ten. Across the top of the first page was scrawled in English, 'Excellent. Brilliant psychological analysis.'

Our relationship underwent a dramatic overhaul. He stopped looking at me with dismissive eyes and I soon became his devoted follower. Instead of staid textbooks, he made us read the *Bhagwat-Gita*, an ancient treatise – a dramatic speech really, given on the battlefield by Lord Krishna – on the subject of duty and action. He had us study the sixteenth-century poet Mira Bai's devotional love songs and Tulsidas's version of the *Ramayana* of the same period. Looking directly at me, he stopped to translate the more difficult Old Hindi words because he knew I would demand an explanation otherwise. Knowing I loved to read, he suggested Hindi novels and poems quite out of our curriculum, such as Premchand's rural novel *Godan* and Harivansh Rai Bachchan's poem about our struggle for independence, *Madhushala*.

Academically at least, I was now riding a crest. I was comfortable in all the subjects needed for high school. English, history and drawing were old friends. Hindi had become an exciting new one. That left only lower mathematics, that combination of arithmetic with domestic science. I could manage the arithmetic, the needlework, the removing of stains, naming all the 206 bones in the human body and tying bandages wherever required. What I absolutely could not stomach was the cookery. Oh yes, I could light a charcoal fire and set a pot on it. What I couldn't bring my body and soul to do was cook the food. The textbooks hadn't changed suddenly after independence. We were still being asked to prepare British invalid foods circa 1930 and not much else. Blancmange still loomed large.

The foods I actually ate at school lunchtimes were far more tantalizing. They had changed considerably since Partition. My new friends were bringing foods from much further afield. Manoranjana brought very thick, large, earthy Punjabi village *parathas* (griddle breads) stuffed with white radish. The accompanying condiment was a rough-cut, sweet-sour pickle made with *jaggery* (raw brown sugar) and mustard-laced cauliflower, turnip and carrot. Another new student, Leela, a Syrian Christian from the southern state of Kerala, intrigued us with her food, *idlis* (steamed rice cakes) and coconut chutney flecked with whole brown mustard seeds. She left us with our mouths agape as she described her tropical home state which none of us had visited. 'There are coconut palms everywhere,' she said, 'and we all – everyone, rich and poor – walk barefoot as the roads are so clean ...' A second, even more orthodox Jain girl from Rajasthan, also named Sudha, brought just boiled potatoes and some mixed spices in a newspaper packet. As we watched, she peeled the potatoes and crushed them coarsely. She then opened her newspaper packet, lifted some spice mixture with the tips of her fingers and sprinkled it over the potatoes. I was never able to work out what that magical mixture was. I have not been able to re-create it, perhaps because it has attained mythical proportions in my head. Her potatoes were divine.

CHAPTER TWENTY-FIVE

Exam Season ❉ *Brain Food* ❉ *The Honey-seller*
Sweetening the Mouth

As soon as I got home from school, hot and sweaty from cycling, my mother would produce cold *phirni* from the refrigerator. This was a very light, cardamom-scented pudding made with coarsely ground rice that my mother set in shallow terracotta bowls (*shakoras*). A layer of *varak*, real silver tissue, was laid over the surface and pistachios, slivered into *havaiyan*, airy nothings, sprinkled over the top. I would slide the spoon in and begin eating. The sweet, cool, milky pudding, tasting of the cardamom and pistachios with an earthy aroma of terracotta, went down smoothly. It was worlds away from the blancmange!

There was no time to rest afterwards. May was the time for our annual exams and all of April had to be spent doing revision. Indian history was the most demanding as it started in the early BCs. Battles, sieges, dates, planting of trees, emperors, ever-changing maps, kingdoms expanding and contracting, planting of trees, new laws, statutes, declarations, acts passed, planting of trees . . . Indian emperors planted a lot of trees, probably for the shade they provided. We always seemed to be writing sentences like, 'King Ashoka gave alms to the poor, spread Buddhism and planted many trees . . .' The British history textbook was somewhat thinner. As I struggled to retain the causes of the War of the Roses or remember the cast of

I pose by the neem tree at Number 5, aged about sixteen.

characters championing the Spanish Armada, my mother brought me cooling glasses of *chha*, buttermilk flavoured with salt and roasted cumin.

While I studied in my hot back room, my mother sat knitting for my sisters in their frigid Himalayan convent. In the superheated Delhi of April, I could hardly even look at wool, let alone touch it. My mother just carried on heroically.

Each examination was three hours long, starting and ending promptly at the designated time. On most days there were two exams with a break for lunch. Before I left early in the morning, armed with sharpened pencils, pens freshly filled with ink, ink bottles, rulers and erasers, my mother would appear with a plate containing two almond balls (*badaam ki goli*). She made these by soaking the nuts overnight, peeling them, then grinding them with sugar and cardamom, forming soft balls, and finally covering the balls with silver tissue. They were the most elegant snack you could ever hope to see. My mother firmly believed that almonds were brain food and that any child sent off to write two examination papers for six hours unfortified with almond balls was surely suffering from the grossest form of neglect. I would take a bite of the *badaam ki goli* and savour it on my tongue. Meanwhile my mind would be thinking . . . there are 1760 yards to a mile, that's 5280 feet to a mile . . .

Blank sheets were handed out and we began. Teachers patrolled the rooms to catch cheaters. I wrote as fast as I could, barely stopping to think. I would lift up a hand, 'More paper please,' and keep writing. Most questions, except, of course, for arithmetic, had to be answered in an essay form. For example, the question, 'What were the causes, main events and results of the battle of Panipat?' would require regurgitating a couple of chapters I had crammed about the founding of the Moghul empire, with all relevant dates duly stated. There was no sliding into fiction here.

I would return home, ink-stained and exhausted, and immediately begin studying for the next day's exams. My mother never asked me how I had fared. She always assumed that I would do well.

Often she would try and distract me from my studies if she thought I was working too hard. One afternoon, when the servants were off-duty, she called me saying, 'Come, come, there is a man here selling honey.' By the time I came out, the man was well into his sales pitch ... 'Purer honey than this you can never hope to find. Look at its fine golden colour. See, see, it still has pieces of honeycomb suspended in the middle. Smell it. The odour of nature's flowers . . .' My mother cut right to the chase, 'But how do I know it is pure? What proof do you have?' She was hoping she had stumped him.

He turned out to be wilier than that. 'What proof, you want to know? The oldest proof in the world. It has worked since the beginning of time. First you catch a fly and then you throw it into the honey. It will sink. If the honey is impure, it will keep sinking and die. If the honey is pure, it will rise to the surface and fly away.' At that he swung his hand in the air and caught a fly, flinging it immediately into the honey. It sank. Then it started to rise, higher and higher until it reached the surface and flew away. My mother was so impressed, she bought several jars and I went back to my studies.

That evening, when our cook returned from his afternoon break and my mother recounted the honey story, he said, '*Arey Memsa'ab* [Oh lady], you have been completely duped. I can do exactly the same thing with sugar syrup.' Our cook seemed as adept at catching flies with his hand as the honey man. He caught one and threw it into a jar of sugar syrup that my mother kept for sweetening our fresh lime juice. The fly sank, then rose to the top and flew away. We teased our mother mercilessly.

Soon after the exams, the results were announced. If they were good, it necessitated an immediate mango and ice cream party, sometimes with *rasgullas* (cheese balls in syrup) as well. As it was the height of summer, it also meant that it was the height of the mango season. Our grandparents, as well as our neighbouring aunts, uncles and cousins, were immediately summoned for a celebratory 'sweetening-of-the-mouth'. My mother never called this simply a party. Sweetening the mouth was auspicious and had the hallowed ring of tradition to it. A party was just a party. 'Come around five, five-thirty?' my mother would say.

Boxes of mangoes were hurriedly sent for from a Kashmiri Gate fruit stall. *Rasgullas* came in terracotta crocks from Bengali Market – Bengalis made this sweet better than anyone else – and three-flavoured, three-coloured blocks of strawberry, chocolate and vanilla ice cream from Kwality's in New Delhi. Before Partition, our thick, creamy, homemade ice cream had come from a small Muslim, family-run restaurant in Kashmiri Gate named Idris, after its owner. We could actually taste its main ingredient, clotted cream (*malai*). But that was all in the past. We couldn't linger on what used to be.

We would all bathe and change. The women wore flowing white voile sarees, especially embroidered for them in Lucknow with white thread. Jasmine from the garden – also white and fragrant with summer's promises – was the only ornamentation in the hair. The men wore similarly embroidered white *kurtas*. As the party started, a mother whose child had scored particularly spectacular marks would try to dull her eyes with feigned clouds of humility. 'Have more mango,' she would say to her guests.

As good ripe mangoes were full of juice, there was a simple trick – now well mastered – of eating them without squirting our crisp white clothing with orange. You just had to lean over your plate and have napkins handy.

CHAPTER TWENTY-SIX

*First Jobs and First Loves ❋ Ballroom Dancing
Dressing for the Dinner Dance*

Amid all the changes we had experienced since Independence and Partition, our social life was evolving too. Not mine, really, as I was still in school and destined to remain a mere voyeur for a while, but that of my older brothers, sisters and cousins. The first year that followed independence had been full of elation and sorrows but Delhi had settled down and was in a celebratory mood.

My brothers were now out of college and starting their first jobs. My elder brother, Brijdada, was working at the same cloth mill as my father. Bhaiyyadada – devastatingly handsome, at least in my eyes, and puckish in his humour – had tried to join the Indian army after his Masters degree and had undergone several of their tests. I understood why he might want to join. National feelings were running high. India had been forcibly truncated and felt embattled and threatened. China loomed to the northeast; Pakistan gnawed at the northwest. I didn't want him to go into the army. With belligerence between India and Pakistan soaring, I wanted him at home. In the end, he joined Shibbudada's very successful firm as second in command. It seemed a natural extension of their relationship, which had remained close and trusting through the years.

Me with Lalit, some friends and Lalit's future husband Madan (far right) on the wall of the beer garden at the Cecil Hotel, Simla, three years after Partition.

My older siblings and cousins were of an age to fall in love or at least to have deep emotional leanings. They were living up to expectations. Since we – the younger generation and our friends – did everything together as a large, friendly gang, it was hard at first for me to comprehend that stronger, more intimate relationships might be forming among those in our midst. Since such things were never discussed, I had to keep my antennae up and focused.

My grandfather still insisted that we all come over to Number 7 for a meal every day, dinner, breakfast or lunch. If we had friends visiting, it was expected that we would just bring them along. We never knew who might be filling up the benches in the dining room when we arrived. Other than the assorted first, second, third and fourth cousins, there were all their college friends who came and went too. Sometimes there were so many people, we had to eat in relays. Our picnics now comprised just the younger set and were frequently thought up on the spur of the moment. No demands were made on any household kitchen as there was no long-term planning. All of us – brothers, sisters, friends and cousins of assorted ages – would pack into cars, pick up food from Moti Mahal and drive off to the same historic sites or dammed rivers we were already familiar with. Only this time all participants were young and included refugee college-mates for whom Delhi was new.

Even visits to the hills – to Simla, for example – might be under-taken by a similar collection of siblings, cousins and friends. Instead of renting houses, we just stayed at a hotel.

Who was developing feelings for whom? Love, or something like it, seemed to be blooming right before my eyes. It was quite clear that Lalit and a student at St Stephen's College, a tall Hindu from northwestern Pakistan called Madan, were getting close. They went for walks together. Among the refugee friends he had introduced to us was a young girl from Karachi whom Bhaiyyadada seemed to like. Lalit's best friend at college, a young Kashmiri girl, had a brother who seemed to dote on my cousin, Toshijiji, whom we called Tosh. Tosh and her family had been living in Lahore at the time of Partition and had been forced to flee. All round me there was an entanglement of relationships, bubbling and heaving with varying degrees of intensity.

One Holi I discovered that my dear sister Kamal was perhaps developing a crush as well. A handsome youth visited frequently. I noticed that whenever he walked by our house he whistled a jaunty tune which ended after he'd passed our second gate. He was a good whistler.

That Holi had been like any other, a free-for-all with cousins, friends, aunts and uncles all participating in assorted high jinks, and most ending up in the tank of *tesu* water. I watched this youth circle Kamal and then grab her and rub red powder all over her face. She laughed and covered his face in return with the golden paste she was carrying in a jar. She seemed to be anointing him. Their play was innocent and yet I could sense their attraction. Of course Kamal didn't say one word to me about it.

Shibbudada's eldest son was studying statistics in America. He had met an American girl and there was talk of a marriage. Sheila, Shibbudada's daughter, was meant to be in love with an economics professor at Delhi University. Was it true? It was all hush-hush as the gentleman in question, it was said, already had a wife in Kashmir.

I watched and listened as I felt attractions and tensions straining the air but I stayed at arm's length. Sometimes my brothers, sisters and their friends would go dancing at the clubs. They had already started dance lessons with a Madame Varda who was reputed to have Russian blood. What Madame Varda taught them was nothing particularly Russian. It was ballroom dancing that was highly popular at the time, the rumba, tango, quickstep and the waltz – both the slow one and the fast-twirling Viennese. When they came home from their lesson, my brothers and sisters danced with each other, winding up their gramophone and dancing to 78-inch records of Victor Sylvester and his Band. They had become very good by now. Bhaiyyadada and Lalit were particularly smooth at the tango, holding each other tightly, their feet swaying and sliding.

I would hear them make reservations for a Saturday dinner

dance. Dinner jackets would be sent out for pressing to the *dhobi* (laundryman). My sisters would look through their sarees again and again. Would something they already owned suffice or did they need to go shopping? By now they had starting wearing sarees frequently, both for everyday and formal wear. We had been convinced, mostly by Lalit who guided our tastes, that ordinary silks were common and bourgeois. We were to wear rare, handloom cottons, some from far-off villages, others distinguished by fine work in real gold thread. In the summer, only the sheerest cream *Chanderis*, see-through cotton and silk mixtures from Central India, would do. If silk was to be worn at all, then it had to be some exquisite antique, perhaps once worn in South Indian temples by nineteenth-century dancing girls. When a new saree was purchased, it didn't come with a matching blouse. The blouse would need to be sewn and Ram Narain, our tailor, hurriedly sent for.

It was equally gauche to wear any of my mother's heavy jewellery. Only small, rare pieces were stylish. We went to the jewellers again and again with our mother, searching through their storage boxes for old Moghul titbits. There was the tiger's claw we found, set in the most delicate gold filigree, which could be strung and worn around the neck. Then there was the *hauldali*. Years later, when we were old enough to have our own children, my mother – smart woman that she was – decided to distribute all her sarees, shawls and jewellery between her daughters while she was still alive. The two things we all wanted were the green *jamevaar* shawl and this *hauldali*.

The *hauldali* was a white jadeite tablet set with precious stones arranged in a delicate floral pattern, each flower and leaf outlined with gold. Its workmanship was not unlike that of Emperor Shah Jahan's wine cup, now in London's Victoria and Albert Museum. My mother had it strung with a simple black thread so it could be worn modestly around the neck. (Veena got the *jamevaar*, I have the *hauldali*.)

The great hullabaloo in the days preceding a dinner dance had me all worked up too. I couldn't go but at least I could watch my sisters dress. They sat in their petticoats and blouses before my mother's three-mirrored dressing table and put on their make-up – nothing much, just some rouge and lipstick and a little kohl on the eyes. They coiffed their hair in buns. If any hair ornaments were to be worn, they would consist of jasmine from the garden, made into a thick rope wound around the bun. Heels were out. Gauche, gauche. It was only proper to wear flat *chappals* (slippers), perhaps the natural leather ones from Kohlapur in Maharashtra. Finally the saree, all ironed by the *aayaa*, was wound around and my sisters were ready. How very beautiful they were.

My brothers, smelling of Old Spice, drove off into the night with my jasmine-scented sisters. They would meet their friends and eat and dance. I wanted so much to grow up fast but was afraid I would never end up with their grace or looks.

When they returned late at night, I was up and waiting. They would talk among themselves and I would listen. Lalit, the joy of the evening still singing inside her, would say merrily, 'You want to dance? I'll teach you.' She would take hold of me as if she were the man. 'Here we go. This is the waltz . . . *one* two three, *one* two three . . . dip and take a long slide on the *one*,' or 'Here is the quickstep. Forward, quick-quick slow; backward, quick-quick slow.' We would practise, she leading me around the bedroom furniture, twirling and sliding until we fell down on the bed in a heap of giggles.

CHAPTER TWENTY-SEVEN

Future Planning ✳ *The Radio Station* ✳ *The Last Large Picnic*
Wildflower Hall and an Encounter with the Police

I was happy enough in my last years at school, but something deep inside me knew that the life I was living wasn't my real life. I was convinced that I belonged in another world. I had no idea what that world might be. I just knew I hadn't found it yet. One day it would happen. I would step out of one life and into another one, the one I was meant to be in. I was oddly calm and optimistic about it.

I had begun thinking about college and what I might want to do with my life. I thought I wanted to be a painter and that I would apply to the J.J. School of Art in Bombay (now Mumbai).

Naturally, I discussed this with Lalit. 'You could do that,' she said, in her thoughtful, practical way, 'But why not go to J.J. later? Go to a regular college now and get a proper BA degree, and once you have that as a backup, you can do anything else you want.'

It seemed far too practical. I just wanted to fly away somewhere, quickly, and paint with blobs of oil paint.

'Get a degree in what? What else am I interested in?' I wanted to know.

'You could do an honours in English,' Lalit suggested. Lalit and Sheila were studying English at college. 'That's my subject. It's Sheila's too. Or you could do history like K.'

Me and Lalit (right) on the gate of Number 5.

Kamal attended a new, all-girls college that had just opened, Miranda House. All its brick buildings were not yet fully in place. It had become a highly desirable destination for Delhi's graduating schoolgirls, partly because it was just behind the hallowed St Stephen's College (now going through a males-only phase) and partly because it had begun to attract the brightest young ladies in town.

Unfortunately, Miranda House, just like all Delhi's colleges, was bound by Delhi University rules and offered a most limited range of subjects. In the Arts category (mathematics and the sciences were obviously quite out of the question for me) we could do an honours degree in English, Hindi, history, philosophy or economics, with a subsidiary in one other of the same subjects. Or we could get a general BA degree in some of these subjects without specializing in any of them. The general degree carried much less cachet. I postponed thinking about it. I didn't have to apply to any college until after I'd graduated from school. The J.J. School of Art seemed to be drifting further and further away.

I had started taking on odd jobs at All India Radio. Delhi's first radio station was barely five minutes away from Number 7. Even as a young child I was quite familiar with the soft thump of recording-studio doors and the musty, enclosed smell of radio-station corridors. Whenever children were required for radio plays or children's programmes, our gang of cousins was summoned. Where else could just one phone call produce such a variety of children, all of whom could be counted on to read fluently and 'with expression'? The call always came to Number 7, to the one phone there located in a corner of the gallery. Whoever answered it then pigeonholed a servant and asked him to do the rounds of all the surrounding houses to convey the relevant information.

I had been taking part in radio plays almost since I could read. Now that independent India's new All India Radio had been established in New Delhi, I was asked to come in several times a year. As I was paid a small fee for each session, this could be considered my first professional work. It felt more like play than work. A car was sent to pick me up; I met other school children I'd never seen before; we were offered tea and samosas; then we stood around a microphone and read our lines while invisible goblins in the recording booth made sounds of doors closing, cars starting, thunder and rain. We knew how to dip our knees slightly and drop the page we had just finished onto the floor without a rustle and to refrain from fidgeting noisily while someone else was reading. Radio was fun – and easy. Already, the allure of work that felt like play had begun to infiltrate my being.

My grandfather, far too old to work now, had stopped his annual trips to Simla some time back, but we still went. Sometimes we would go to Simla and sometimes to other hill stations; sometimes with elders of our parents' generation and sometimes without. I hardly knew where I belonged. At Hackman's Hotel in the hill station of Mussoori, I sometimes felt grown-up enough to attend the dinner dances there with my older brothers and sisters, to eat the never-before-tasted cream cheese on crisp-breads as I watched scantily dressed European cabaret artists slither along the dance floor to the glow of a spotlight. At other times, though, I just felt too awkward in my glasses and pigtails and chose to skip these evenings and to accompany my mother on her shop-ping expeditions the following morning instead.

All major *saree* shops had branches in hill resorts. My mother was their much-welcomed patron. I would sit with her for hours at Leela Ram and Sons as she examined bolts of French chiffon. In chiffons, she never seemed to pick pure colours. She might choose a blue with a hint of silver, a salmon pink dulled with grey or a maroon so dark it was almost brown. Then she looked for match-ing borders, thick Benarasi brocaded borders that came like a roll of wide ribbon, made with real gold and silver thread. She laid one border after another on the chosen chiffons to see how well they matched. Once the decisions were made, she still couldn't take anything home. The borders needed to be sewn on to the delicate chiffons by hand. Fabrics for the blouses and petticoats had to be picked out and then everything left at Leela Ram's for stitching and finishing.

We hadn't stopped going on our hill picnics but, just like in the city, their character had changed. The older generation, if they were in the hills with us at all, stayed at home now, exerting themselves just enough with gentle strolls and shopping on the Mall. It was the youngsters who picnicked. One year in Simla, about eighteen of us decided to create our own kind of picnic by cycling from Simla to Mashobra, a good eight miles away, all of them uphill. The group ranged in age from mid-twenties down to me, the youngest, still at school. It included college mates of my brothers and cousins, lovers, friends and relatives. Our destination was at least 1000 feet higher than Simla, standing at 8250 feet above sea level.

Mashobra was a tiny hill town on the India–Tibet Road. Now part of the national Simla Reserve Forest Sanctuary, it was always devastatingly beautiful. High up on a spur that fell down sharply into deep valleys, it was ringed by snow-covered peaks. Its glades were massed with wild flowers, its steeply sloping sides thick with deodars (Himalayan cedars), oaks, pines and rhododendrons where pheasants, musk deer, partridges and eagles darted, leapt and soared. There were plenty of gushing streams for those who wanted to wet their feet and orchards for those hungry for apples or apricots plucked straight from the trees.

All members of my family knew Mashobra well. We had picnicked and trekked there year after year. Aside from simple local dwellings, there were a few remaining turn-of-the-century British homes from the Raj days, the most famous of which was Wildflower Hall. Built originally in 1866, it had become a cooling haven for the rest and recreation of British India's rulers, its viceroys and commanders-in-chief. Lady Dufferin, writing in her book, *Our Viceregal Life in India*, declares, 'This country villa of ours is 1000 feet higher than Simla. It is on top of a hill and in the midst of the most sweet-smelling pinewoods where the mountain views are magnificent.'

Wildflower Hall's most famous resident in the early part of the twentieth century was Lord Kitchener, the great warrior of Khartoum. Indians referred to him as the *Jungy Laat Sa'ab* or the Warrior Lord Sahib. Having made a name for himself in North Africa, he had been posted to India as commander-in-chief. Thwarted in his hopes of being appointed viceroy, he found great solace and comfort in Wildflower Hall where he gardened and worked on an ingenious ice pit. Winter snow was pushed into a dark, covered hole and left there all through the frigid months. By the summer its own weight had converted it into ice, which could then be used by the Wildflower Hall kitchen for the rest of the year.

Kitchener left India in 1909. Wildflower Hall was sold to a hotelier whose wife eventually tore it down and built a hotel with the same name in 1925. It was considered quite grand for its time. This was the hotel we had known and frequented. Our family had grown up with it. We often stopped there for lunch or tea when we were out on family treks or picnics. We wanted to show it off to our new friends.

That day, we rented our bicycles, picked up some sandwiches and drinks and, in one large group of wild cyclists, left Simla through the Sanjauli tunnel.

We would have to cycle uphill for most of the outward journey. That hardship seemed a fair trade for the return trip, which we knew would be a joyous glide home. We pushed our pedals and sweated along the hairpin bends, all stubbornly pointed upwards, stopping often to drink at small waterfalls. When we reached Wildflower Hall, we found it eerily quiet. All the vegetation seemed unkempt and overgrown. We tried a door. It was locked. We knocked. Where was everybody? We tried another door. It too was locked. We so wanted our new friends to see our beloved Wildflower that one of us probably pushed on a door too hard and it flew open. We all entered a familiar dining room, happy and laughing. It was then that a few caretakers approached us. They accused us of breaking into the hotel, which was now closed, and told us to wait right where we were as they had called the police.

The police, when they arrived, were in no mood to accept any explanations or protestations of innocence. We, with our bicycles, were loaded into the back of an open truck for an immediate trip back to the Sanjauli police station. 'Couldn't we return on our bicycles and meet you at the police station?' we asked, thinking of the downhill ride we were being deprived of. They were unrelenting.

We sat in the police station for hours, answering the same questions again and again until it was dark. What had seemed quite funny was now getting seriously worrisome. At that stage it occurred to one of our friends that he was closely related to a very senior member of the Himachal State government. He made a telephone call, which was followed almost instantly with apologies and release.

This was possibly our last large picnic. The number of attendees had been dwindling. In posed photographs of family picnics taken at the turn of the century, there were 300 or more formally dressed family members, with my grandfather and his brothers seated grandly on chairs in the centre. Later photographs showed forty or fifty people, then thirty, then twenty. We were all growing up and our lives were never going to be the same.

CHAPTER TWENTY-EIGHT

*Kamal's Journey ❊ Shibbudada Interferes Again
Failing My Cookery Exam*

As Kamal was coming to the end of her second year in college, her leg – the same left ankle – began troubling her again. My parents were distraught. Fresh x-rays were taken and sent off by air to Harley Street specialists in London and the Memorial Sloan-Kettering Cancer Care Center in New York. One biopsy after another was done and these results, too, were sent abroad. The specialists suspected a bone tumour but wanted to examine her before recommending a clear course of action. She needed to go to the West.

Shibbudada thundered back into the centre of our lives. Perhaps he had never left. *He* would take her. Raghudada, his eldest son, had recently married the American girlfriend we'd been hearing about. Shibbudada could now meet the new bride, Thelma, and also make sure that Kamal's medical problems were thoroughly examined. He made the decision and it was not questioned.

I don't know how my father felt about this arrangement. He certainly said nothing, though his eyes looked more lost than ever. And what did Shibbudada's wife and children think? Not a word was uttered. We all seemed deeply unsettled, though not perhaps for the same reasons.

While preparations were being made for Kamal's long journey –

My father and mother prepare to say goodbye to Kamal (her arm linked to my father) as she sets off for Europe in search of medical treatment. Shibbudada stands behind my mother.

we weren't at all sure what its duration might be – I was getting ready for my final school exams.

The hot *loo* winds blew viciously that year. I hid in my back room, working hard on my revision. My mother came in daily with a plate holding two beautiful *badaam ki golis*. We said little, just quietly dripped our salty tears over the sweet almond balls. Every evening, just as it became tolerable to leave the air-cooled house, I went outside and picked some jasmine flowers. With a needle and thread, I strung them into a thick rope. I kept this rope near me as I worked. Its aroma, filled with the India I knew, wiped out the rest of the world.

My mother pulled Kamal's warm clothes out of mothballs. Her coats and cardigans were aired. New silk *sarees* were bought as it was thought that crushable cottons, which could be worn just once before needing special cleaning, light starching and ironing, would be most impractical, however much we loved them. Kamal already had several pairs of slacks but more were sewn. My mother was learning. This was her first child to leave for distant shores. When Lalit and I left some years later, she would know exactly what to do.

My exam time arrived while our hearts were focused on Kamal. I had been able to concentrate on my work through the wretched years of Partition and I must have done so again as I had no difficulties with the English, Hindi, history or drawing tests. Lower mathematics, my *bête noire*, proved the most exacting exam, but for reasons I could hardly have anticipated.

I had worked at the arithmetic up, down, across and sideways. I had practised every possible type of sum or problem that could be thrown at me. I had done it once, twice and thrice. When the exam questions were put before me, they seemed quite accessible. I finished the exam and checked my answers a dozen times, handing in my paper well before my three hours were up. When the results came, I had some of the highest marks in arithmetic.

It was domestic science that let me down.

When I arrived for the 'practical' test, there were no stains for me to clean, no herringbone stitches for me to do on a small piece of cloth and no bandages to tie. I was a master at bandages. I could crisscross them over the head or the ankle to perfection.

For this test, we were all asked to congregate in what appeared to be the dusty ruins of some old municipal property, not at all encouraging for my morale. Then all the hapless students were led to a dark corner where, piled on the floor, were sacks of potatoes, tomatoes, onions, garlic, ginger and assorted spices.

'Use these ingredients to cook a dish. Here are the matches. Here is the wood. Now …. go.'

Go where? Excuse me, what happened to the blancmange?

Over the next few years, I tried to understand what might have transpired on that disastrous day. Some wise-guy examiner must have said, 'Why are we asking these poor Indian children to cook something they have never eaten, like this boring European blanc-mange? Why don't we ask them to cook some everyday Indian food, like simple potatoes?'

But to change course without any notice? For someone like me who couldn't cook at all, it was a frightening proposition. Given a chance to prepare, I might have worked on a few Indian dishes. But, just when I had mastered every last detail of British invalid cookery circa 1930, why were we being presented with Indian spices?

I did the best I could. I cut up everything I found – potatoes, onion, garlic, ginger, tomatoes, chillies and green coriander – into even-sized pieces and threw them into a pot with a little water. I sprinkled a few spices and salt over the top, put the lid on as I couldn't bear to look at my bubbling creation, and prayed. It did no good. The only reason I passed lower mathematics was because my marks for arithmetic were so high that they made up for the cooking I must have failed.

I did well enough in the other subjects to pass school in the first division (the top grade). I applied for admission to Miranda House, Kamal's college, and in my form stated that I wished to do an Honours degree in English with a subsidiary in philosophy.

Meanwhile, Kamal and Shibbudada got on a plane and flew to London.

CHAPTER TWENTY-NINE

A Joint Family in New York ❋ *Grandfather's Decline*
A Riverside Cremation

During the long, hot summer of 1950 we stayed in Delhi to await letters, telegrams, phone calls, any communication from abroad. The news from the first stop, London, was not heartening. The Harley Street specialists seemed to confirm the Indian diagnosis: bone cancer. New York was the next stop. Sloan-Kettering doctors agreed and suggested two long sessions of radiation treatment.

Kamal and Shibbudada, who had been staying at New York's Barbizon Plaza Hotel for the first month, now needed to find longer-term accommodation. Shibbudada decided to rent a large house in flushing, Queens, where there would be room enough for Raghudada and his new wife, Thelma, for Thelma's mother, Kamal and himself. He was creating a little joint family in New York.

Thelma's mother and Thelma did most of the cooking. Kamal's letters were full of praise for them and the new foods appearing daily at the table. She seemed particularly enamoured of upside-down cakes and whole hams glazed with pineapple. We couldn't even imagine what they might taste like.

In Delhi my grandfather, now in his late eighties and already enfeebled, took a turn for the worse. Until then he had used a walking stick to help ease himself first onto the front verandah and then onto the Number 7 front lawn in the evenings. Here he enjoyed the few passing breezes, smoked his hookah and drank his whisky. Of late he had felt too weak to make this effort. He chose to stay in his room, generally in his bed. He soon began complaining of the heat. Large ice blocks were sent for and spread under and around his bed. I remember taking my shoes off and sloshing into his room to give him a kiss. A haze rose from the ice. My grandfather looked so thin. Several women in their white summer sarees hovered around him.

Soon he was unable to get out of the bed at all and seemed to be asleep most of the time. The doctor, the same S.B. Mathur who had pierced my ears, recommended an oxygen mask. The women were taking turns to hold it up to his face. He was kept in his room during the heat of the day, but if the evening was reasonably cool, the entire setup – the bed with my grandfather in it *and* his oxygen tank – was carried out to the lawn.

One day, when it was my mother's turn to hold the oxygen mask, she beckoned to me and said, 'I have to run to the kitchen. Could you take over for a few minutes?'

My hand replaced my mother's. The mask stayed over my grandfather's sleeping face. I must have got distracted and shifted my position as I felt my grandfather raise his arm and, with a powerful move, pull my hand back into place. Although he was dying, this once-powerful man was not going to go easily.

Kamal and Shibbudada on their grand tour of Europe,
travelling in style to Britain on board the RMS Queen Mary.

Kamal had begun her first radiation treatment but her letters remained upbeat. They were not going to return directly, she wrote. Shibbudada was going to take her on a grand tour of Europe first. They would sail from New York on the *Queen Mary*, stay in London at Grosvenor House, then travel to Paris, Rome . . .

Shibbudada, just like all of us, was worried about her future and was offering her the world now. He seemed determined to keep her smiling.

My grandfather continued to deteriorate. One day as I cycled into Number 7, I saw small groups of people walking silently towards the house. He must have died, I thought. I berated myself for not having been with him at the time but told myself that he wouldn't have noticed anyway.

He lay on his bed with his eyes closed. The sunlight coming in through the window was making strange shapes on his chalky face. His arms, lying outside the top sheet, were covered to the wrist with the crisp starched sleeves of a muslin *kurta* (shirt). The hands – those aristocratic hands with the long tapering fingers and perfectly oval nails, hands inherited by my father and most of my father's children, except me – were facing down in a slightly cupped position.

I could hear my father and eldest uncle, Taoji, talking.

'We must send for the barber.'

'The body must be bathed . . .'

'. . . and put on the floor. Shall we use the big room?'

'That will be best . . . There will be so many people.'

Most men had their personal barbers to cut and shape their hair, but in our family we also had ceremonial barbers. A ceremonial barber had many functions, some involving hair and some not. This gentleman was an official matchmaker and carrier of horoscopes, a service he had performed for my parents. He was also responsible for shaving the head of the oldest son of a deceased father in a semi-religious ceremony. It was only after this purifying shaving had taken place that the oldest son could light the funeral pyre, as custom demanded.

A chair was put on the lawn. My uncle sat down and the razor approached his head. He just stared at the grass.

The big room, across the gallery from the drawing room, was cleared and cleaned. Once he had been bathed, my grandfather was moved there and laid on the floor on a clean sheet. He was now in a fresh *kurta* with mother-of-pearl buttons. Relatives and friends began to congregate, sitting down cross-legged on the floor all around the body. Some dabbed their eyes; others talked. They filled up the room, even overflowing on to the front and side verandahs and the gardens beyond.

The cremation had to take place that very day so there was no time to dally. The body was enshrouded in a white sheet and the sheet secured. As Babaji was being lifted onto a bier, my father, who until then had been performing his tasks perfunctorily and quietly, let out two deep, echoing sobs, like a wounded animal. Then he abruptly collected himself and went on with the business of tying the body to the bier. But the escaped sobs, like large waves, reverberated through the big room, through the verandahs and out across the lawn. Everywhere they passed there was sobbing and wailing.

Then the two sons who were present and two grandsons heaved the bier up onto their shoulders and began walking in the direction of the river. We followed, chanting:

Ram nam Satya hai
Satya bolo, Satya hai
(The only truth is God's name
Speak truth for truth is)

Normally, only men went to the riverside cremation grounds. But we were considered a very 'modern' family, known for changing the rules. After all, had not Rai Bahadur Raj Narain sent his own daughters to St Stephen's College? Still, the older generation of women, following older rules, stayed home. But we youngsters followed the bier.

At the cremation grounds the body was put down several times so priests could chant and pray over it. After a final, purifying immersion in the Yamuna River, the bier was placed on the sandal-wood pyre. Incense and perfumes were sprinkled and more wood piled on top to form a 'roof'. My eldest, shaved, uncle was handed a torch to set the pyre aflame.

On the third day the family returned to 'gather the flowers'. The wood and the body had burnt themselves out. All that was left were bones and ashes. These were to be collected in cloth bags and taken to a holy spot on the Ganges River where they were to be scattered, just as had been done to the remains of all our family members going back thousands of years. Throughout the funeral, I cried only twice. Once when my father released his sobs and then when I came across one unburned mother-of-pearl button among the ashes.

Hindus believe that after thirteen days, the human soul, having fully disentangled itself from the earth, ascends heavenwards to become one with the Universal Soul. Mourning ends. This thirteenth day is celebrated with a family feast.

And what a feast it is. Laid out on the table is a collection of unusually delicious vegetarian foods, all cooked by the family, all prepared according to rules followed only on such a day, rules that seem impossible to fathom. No turmeric, asafetida, garlic or onions could be used. When preparing the delicate rice pudding, *kheer*, the rice first had to be stir-fried in a teaspoon of *ghee* (clarified butter). *Urad dal* (a split pea of Indian origin) was required to make an appearance in as many incarnations as possible, in stuffings, dumplings, sweets ...

I didn't care about the rules. All I knew was that my grand-father's thirteenth day feast, as befitted the man we were celebrating, was nothing short of spectacular. Most of our aunts, uncles and cousins had trooped into the long, river-facing dining room and gathered around the tables. The green pumpkin – cooked with cloves, fennel and fenugreek – was impossible to ignore. I returned to it again and again, wrapping little morsels in delicate *pooris* (puffed, fried breads) and devouring them hastily. The potatoes, made mainly with ginger, tomatoes and cumin, were simple yet extraordinary – earthy, gingery and hot. There were slim stuffed okra, tiny taro patties smothered with ajowan seeds, meltingly soft *urad dal* dumplings in yoghurt (*dahi baras*), a salad of grated white radish (*churri*) and assorted desserts, including the rice pudding. I ate and ate until I could eat no more. I then got on my bicycle and rushed to Number 5 where I immediately started a letter to Kamal to give her *our* news.

EPILOGUE

Kamal's Return ✳ *A Gift of Coca-Cola* ✳ *Sailing to a New Life*
Mingling the Flavours of the Past and the Future

Kamal returned with suitcases full of fashionable gifts for all of us. I received a pair of calf-length pedal-pushers and a black-and-white striped tee-shirt that practically became my uniform. She also presented me with a light tartan shawl and a sterling silver charm bracelet with the Eiffel Tower dangling from it.

My sister's medical saga, though, was not over. The Indian doctors discovered that Kamal didn't have cancer after all but fibrous dysplasia, a decalcification of the bone that could be cured – could always have been cured – with a simple graft. She went on yet another journey, this time to Bombay, accompanied by my father and Bhaiyyadada. Again, we waited by the telephone. The call came. It was too late. The many radiation sessions had completely destroyed her skin and flesh. The leg would have to be amputated. She was only twenty.

I remember being on a bus that day, returning from college, unable to cope with my feelings of devastation. And yet, I never heard Kamal complain. Just once I saw her weeping silently into the sweet peas as she walked along the Number 5 front wall on her crutches.

Kamal, who so stoically bore her afflictions,
with our brother Bhaiyyadada at Number 5.

I was now seventeen and no longer a child. I went to the Delhi University coffee shop to drink cup after milky cup of sweetened coffee in the company of male friends from the neighbouring St Stephen's College.

One day the largest possible truck stopped outside Number 5. The truck had COCA-COLA emblazoned on it. I thought it was there by mistake. I knew of Coca-Cola only from *Life* magazine and movies. I went up to the gate and asked the driver if he needed help.

Was he at the wrong address? He was at the right address, he said, and looking for me. He said my name and that he was carrying a gift for me from the Coca-Cola Company of America. At this he pulled out dozens of crates and carried them to the house.

I was told I was a 'student leader' and had been selected to receive the gift. I fell for the promotional ruse, throwing party after party to use up my 'gift'. Equating Coke with my new-found internationalism, I took to swigging it from the bottle. I was yet to see the rest of the world but, armed with a pair of pedal-pushers, the charm bracelet and, of course, the Coke, I felt that this phase of my life had to be just around the corner.

Within the next few years my sister Kamal would marry a handsome Gujarati doctor, Hussain, and settle easily into a life of domesticity and children in Delhi. Lalit would marry Madan, her Punjabi fiancé, and move to England where she would spend her life teaching English. Veena stayed in India and continues to sing its praises. Bhaiyyadada married Maya, a beautiful Bengali educated at Smith College in America, and looks out for his sisters. My eldest brother, Brijdada – whose marriage to Asha, Shibbudada's first wife's niece, was arranged by Shibbudada – would be the only one to carry on the ink-pot and quill line, with all the Kayastha tradition in which we were all steeped. As for Shibbudada, he would die suddenly of a penicillin allergy the year I left home, leaving my father and brothers to run his business, and his own children so openly angry that they would start a war and hit out at our family – the only target left – like battering rams, day after day after day . . .

*(Centre) Brijdada and his wife, Asha Bhabi, and their two sons
Anuj (far left) and Atul (far right).*

Lalit and Madan at their wedding reception, held in the garden at Number 7.

Kamal, garlands of jasmine in her hair, with Hussain, on her wedding day.

Kamal with my father on her wedding day.

I appear in The Comedy of Errors *as performed by St Stephen's College.*

Of course, I didn't know all this at the time. I was busy playing Hamlet in an all-women production at college, as well as working in other professional theatrical productions, discovering playwrights such as Jean Paul Sartre, Jean

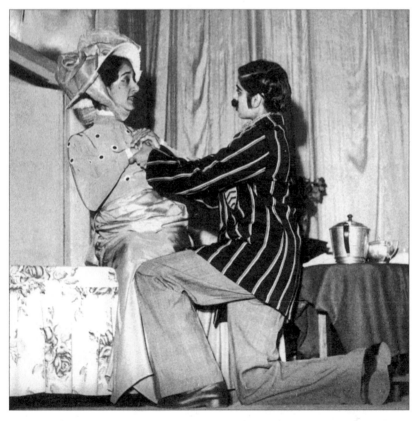

A picture from my college's production – with an all-girl cast – of
The Importance of Being Earnest. *I played Gwendolen.*

Cocteau, Christopher Fry and Tennessee Williams. I was also
busy falling in love. Then, armed with a set of scholarships to the
Royal Academy of Dramatic Art in London, I found myself sailing
due west on a Pacific & Orient ocean liner, all alone but breathless
to taste a new life.

I knew less than the rudiments of cooking then, and found
myself writing home to my mother, begging her to teach me. This
she did, through airmail letters that arrived regularly. I was barely
aware that my old and new worlds would start to mingle as soon as

they touched, and that so much of my past would always remain my present.

The innocent Indian honey of my infancy was now mixed with pungent Indian spices, the sour and bitter, the nutty and the aromatic. Interwoven with these flavours, like tenacious creepers, were births, deaths, illnesses, caste and creed. Yet somewhere in my depths, each bite, each taste of all I had eaten lay catalogued in some pristine file, ready to be drawn up when the moment was ripe.

I graduated from Miranda House, Delhi, in 1953.
My days at drama school were still to come.

FAMILY RECIPES

Phulkas 236

Bimla's Chicken Curry 238

Meatball Curry (Koftas) 240

Maya's Meat and Potatoes (Aloo Gosht) 243

Potatoes with Tomatoes 246

Grandmother's Cauliflower with Cheese 248

Mung Dal with Greens (Alan Ka Saag) 250

Stuffed Okra 252

Chickpea Flour Stew with Dumplings (Karhi) 254

Pumpkin (Kaddu) 257

Yoghurt with Tiny Dumplings (Boondi Ka Dahi) 258

White Radish/Mooli Relish (Churri) 261

Light Rice Pudding (Phirni) 262

Fresh Limeade (Neebu Ka Sharbut) 264

Phulkas

Phulkas were our daily bread. Rather like the chapati for the average north Indian or the tortilla for the Mexican, the flatbread served for our everyday Indian meals was the *phulka*. Closely related to the chapati and made of the same finely ground whole-wheat flour, it could be called its more refined, upper-class cousin. *Phulkas* were smaller, thinner and more delicate.

As we ate our meals, stacks of at least three or four *phulkas* kept appearing from the kitchen, all hot and puffy. As we neared the conclusion of the meal, someone in charge would declare, 'No more *phulkas*!'

Some people like to smear a little butter on their *phulkas* as soon as they are made, but our family generally liked them plain.

Like chapatis, *phulkas* are traditionally made on a *tava* or slightly concave cast-iron griddle, but any cast-iron pan will do. I have taken to using my old pancake pan as the size is right and the pan heats up evenly. A *phulka* spends about 40 seconds on the griddle. Then, in India at least, it is put directly on a hot flame for a few seconds to puff up. I find that this function can be mimicked almost perfectly by a microwave oven. A *phulka* demands two things: the dough should be soft so it remains pliable, and it should cook fast or it will turn hard and brittle.

MAKES 12

250 ml/8 fl oz measure chapati flour (*ata*),
plus more for dusting and rolling

Put the flour in a bowl. Now slowly add water, mixing and kneading as you go, until you have a soft, workable dough. You should need less than 120 ml/4 fl oz water. Knead the dough for 7–8 minutes, then cover with clingfilm or a damp cloth and leave for 30–60 minutes. The dough may also be refrigerated overnight.

When you are ready to eat, put your cast-iron pan on a medium heat and let it sit there for a good 7–8 minutes. Meanwhile, knead your dough again (if it is sticky, flour your hands; if it feels hard, wet your hands) and divide into 12 balls. flour your work surface lightly and roll out one ball into a 13-cm/5¼-inch round, turning it over halfway through the rolling and dusting with flour when necessary. Dust off the flour by slapping it between your hands. Now slap the *phulka* onto the hot griddle for 20 seconds. It should pick up a few brown spots. Turn it over and let it cook for another 20 seconds. The second side should also pick up brown spots. Now lift it up and heat it in the microwave for about 12 seconds on full power. It should puff up.

Put the *phulka* between two plates, the second turned over the first, and make the rest of the *phulkas* the same way. If you don't have a microwave oven, either press down on the *phulka* with a wad of cloth, one section at a time but with speed, or else put it over the medium flame of a second burner for a few seconds.

Bimla's Chicken Curry

This recipe comes from Bimla, who married my cousin Shashi, Saran Bhua's son. The recipe is very like my mother's, only Bimla keeps the sauce thick and clinging to the chicken pieces. It is utterly delicious.

I buy a 1.5-kg/3¼-pound organic chicken and get the butcher to skin it and cut it into small serving pieces. Legs should be separated into drumsticks and thighs, and each breast should be cut into two pieces.

SERVES 4

3 medium onions (about
450 g/1 pound), peeled and
coarsely chopped

20 medium cloves garlic,
peeled and coarsely
chopped

7.5 cm/3 inches fresh ginger,
peeled and chopped

6 tablespoons olive or other
vegetable oil

8 green cardamom pods

2 x 5-cm/2-inch sticks
cinnamon

8 cloves

14 whole peppercorns

1 teaspoon Kashmiri red chilli
powder (or ½ teaspoon
cayenne plus ½ teaspoon of
a nice red paprika)

1 medium chicken, preferably
organic, skinned and cut
into small serving pieces,
net weight about 1.25 kg/
2 pounds 10 ounces

350 ml/12 fl oz rich yoghurt

1½ teaspoons salt or to taste

Put the onions into a blender. Add the garlic and ginger and blend until you have a smooth paste.

Put the oil in a large, heavy sauté or frying pan set over a medium-high heat. When hot, put in the cardamom, cinnamon, cloves and peppercorns. Ten seconds later, add the onion paste and the Kashmiri chilli powder. Now stir-fry for about 10 minutes, turning the heat down to medium, if necessary, until the paste has turned a rich golden brown.

Whenever it seems to stick, sprinkle in a little water and stir it in. Now add the chicken pieces, a few at a time, and stir them in. Again, sprinkle in some water if the sauce sticks to the bottom. When all the chicken has been added, begin to put in the yoghurt, a tablespoon at a time, and stir it in just as you did the water. When the sauce sticks, add yoghurt and stir it in. Do this for about 10–12 minutes. When only 120 ml/4 fl oz of yogurt are left, put it all in and stir it around. Add the salt as well and stir to mix. Now cover, turn the heat to low and cook for 10 minutes, stirring now and then.

Uncover and stir, making sure the sauce is clinging to the chicken.

Meatball Curry

Koftas

These were our everyday meatballs, which could be eaten with rice or *phulkas*. We often took them on train journeys and picnics, when we ate them with *pooris*.

SERVES 4–6

For the Meatballs

450 g/1 pound ground/minced lamb (make sure it's not too fatty)

½ medium onion (about 75 g/2½ oz), peeled and finely chopped

5 cm/2 inches fresh ginger, peeled and grated

3 cloves garlic, peeled and crushed to a pulp

1 tablespoon ground coriander

1¼ teaspoons ground roasted cumin seeds

½ teaspoon Kashmiri red chilli powder

¾ teaspoon salt

3 tablespoons green coriander (cilantro), chopped

1 egg, lightly beaten

Combine all the ingredients for the meatballs, mix well and form 24 meatballs with wetted palms. Arrange the meatballs in a single layer on a plate; cover and refrigerate for at least six hours, preferably overnight.

For the Sauce

5 cm/2 inches fresh ginger,
  peeled and chopped

4–6 cloves garlic, peeled and
  chopped

2 fresh, hot, green chillies

4 tablespoons olive or other
  vegetable oil

2 large black cardamom pods,
  lightly crushed

1 teaspoon whole cumin seeds

4–6 whole cloves

5-cm/2-inch stick of
  cinnamon

4–5 green cardamom pods

2 medium onions (285 g/10
  oz), peeled and finely
  chopped

4 medium tomatoes, grated on
  the coarsest part of a grater,
  or enough to get 350 ml/
  12 fl oz

½ teaspoon Kashmiri red chilli
  powder

4 tablespoons natural (plain)
  yoghurt

¾ teaspoon salt

Make the sauce: put the ginger, garlic and green chillies, along with 3 tablespoons water, into a blender. Blend until you have a smooth paste.

Put the oil in a wide, heavy pan and set over a medium-high heat. When hot, add the black cardamom, cumin, cloves, cinnamon and green cardamom. Stir once or twice and put in the onions. Fry, stirring for about 8 minutes or until the onions are a reddish golden. Add the ginger paste, turning the heat down a little, and stir for 2 minutes. Add the grated tomato and red chilli powder. Stir and cook on a medium-high heat until the tomatoes are reduced to a thick, dark paste and you begin to see the oil.

Turn the heat to medium and add the yoghurt, a tablespoon at a time, until it blends with the sauce. When all the yoghurt has been

added this way, put in 475 ml/16 fl oz/¾ pint water and
the salt. Stir to mix. Slide in the meatballs, making sure they lie in a
single layer, and bring to a simmer. Cover and simmer gently for
50–60 minutes, shaking the pan every now and then and never
stirring with a spoon.

Maya's Meat and Potatoes

Aloo Gosht

Maya, Bhaiyyadada's wife, is the creator of this recipe. In India, this dish is always made with goat. Pieces with bone from the neck and shoulder and marrowbones (which are smaller than lamb marrowbones) are combined with boneless pieces such as those taken from muscles.

You could try making this with goat, which is now widely available in ethnic markets. If you can't get it, you can always fall back on either boneless lamb or a combination of some lamb pieces with bone and others without.

Grating tomatoes is not something that was done at home. I remember watching my mother cook in London when she and my father had come to visit my sister Lalit and me. She put whole, chopped tomatoes into the pan for whatever sauce she was making and then, once the pieces had softened, painstakingly picked off all the skins. It was years later, when I was in the Punjab collecting recipes for a BBC programme, that I learnt this other clever trick that I have used ever since. Tomatoes can be grated on the large, coarse holes of a grater to provide a fresh purée . . . and the skin stays behind. Just hold one side of a tomato against the large holes, push a bit and start grating. Sometimes the coarse skin needs to be cut off but I never bother. I just persist. Keep grating until you have most of the tomato skin left in your hand. Flatten your palm and grate the tomato flesh off the skin.

SERVES 4–6

4 medium, waxy potatoes,
about 350–400 g/13–14 oz

Salt

Ground turmeric

7.5-cm/3-inch piece of fresh
ginger, peeled and chopped

10–12 medium cloves of
garlic, peeled and chopped

Olive or other vegetable oil

8 whole cloves

2 x 5-cm/2-inch sticks of
cinnamon

2 large black cardamom pods,
lightly crushed

2 teaspoons whole cumin
seeds

8 green cardamom pods

2 medium onions (285 g/
10 oz), peeled and very
finely chopped

2 medium tomatoes, grated on
the largest holes of the
grater (you need about
250 ml/8 fl oz)

1½ teaspoons Kashmiri red
chilli powder or ½ teaspoon
cayenne plus 1½ teaspoons
good red paprika

900 g/2 pounds lamb (or
goat), boned or not, and cut
into cubes of about 2.5
cm/1 inch (see above)

1½ teaspoons salt or a bit
more

▲▲▲

Boil the potatoes in their jackets. Allow to cool completely. Peel and cut into halves or quarters, depending on size. You need large, chunky pieces. Rub a little salt and turmeric on them.

Put the ginger, garlic and 4 tablespoons water into a blender. Blend until you have a smooth paste.

Pour about 2 tablespoons oil into a medium, well-used frying pan. Add the potatoes and brown lightly on all sides. Lift carefully out of the oil without breaking them and set aside.

Pour 5 tablespoons oil into a wide, heavy pan and set over a medium-high heat. When hot, add the cloves, cinnamon, black car-damom, cumin seeds and green cardamom. Stir once and put in the onions. Stir-fry for 6–8 minutes or until the onions are golden brown. Add the ginger-garlic paste and fry for another 2 minutes, turning the heat down slightly. Now put in the tomatoes and the Kashmiri chilli powder. Stir and cook on a medium heat until the tomatoes are reduced to a dark paste and the oil begins to show.

Put in the meat. Stir it around for a minute. Add 4 tablespoons water and cover. Cook the meat on a medium heat, stirring now and then, until it has browned a bit. Don't let it burn. Add 350 ml/ 12 fl oz) water and the salt and bring to a boil. Cover and let the meat simmer gently on low heat for 60–80 minutes or until tender (goat takes longer). Add the potatoes and shake the pan. Cover and cook on very low heat for 5 minutes.

Potatoes with Tomatoes

These were our picnic potatoes and the ones we had at special Sunday breakfasts. We ate them with *pooris* or *bedvis*.

SERVES 4–6

6 medium, waxy potatoes, about 600 g/1⅓ pounds

3 tablespoons olive or other vegetable oil

Pinch of ground asafetida

1½ teaspoons whole cumin seeds

½ teaspoon whole fennel seeds

¼ teaspoon whole fenugreek seeds

3 whole, dried, hot red chillies

350 ml/12 fl oz tomatoes, grated on the largest holes of a grater (about 3 medium tomatoes)

1½ teaspoons very finely grated fresh, peeled ginger

1 teaspoon salt, or to taste

Boil the potatoes in their jackets and allow to cool. Peel.

Put the oil in a wide, medium pan and set over a medium-high heat. When hot put in first the asafetida, then the cumin, and finally the fennel, fenugreek and chillies together. Two seconds later, add the grated tomatoes and ginger. Stir-fry until the tomatoes turn a deep red and the oil begins to show, turning down the heat as the cooking progresses so nothing burns. Add 350 ml/12 fl oz water.

Now break the potatoes by hand into pieces that are, very roughly, 0.5-cm/½-inch cubes. They will be all different shapes, but that is the charm of the dish. Add the potato cubes to the pan together with the salt, then stir and bring to a boil. Cover, turn heat to low and cook gently for 12–15 minutes, stirring now and again.

Grandmother's Cauliflower with Cheese

I don't have my grandmother's exact recipe. I never asked her, being too young at the time to know better. But the recipe here is a good approximation (as Jimmy Durante, the American comedian, used to say, 'Da nose knows') and utterly delicious.

Do not use jalapeño or serrano chillies for Indian dishes. They have the wrong texture and flavour. Green bird's-eye chillies or any long, slim, thin-skinned variety such as cayenne are ideal. If you can't find them, use ½–¾ teaspoon cayenne pepper instead of the ¼ teaspoon.

SERVES 4–6

2 tablespoons olive or other vegetable oil

1 teaspoon whole cumin seeds

675 g/1½ pounds medium-sized cauliflower florets, cut so each floret has a stem

400 ml/14 fl oz grated fresh tomato (see page 243)

2.5-cm/1-inch piece of fresh ginger, peeled and grated to a pulp on the finest part of a grater or microplane

2 fresh, hot green chillies, cut into slim rounds

¼ teaspoon cayenne pepper

¼ teaspoon ground turmeric

1 tablespoon ground coriander seeds

¾ teaspoon salt or to taste

4 tablespoons chopped fresh green coriander (cilantro)

3 tablespoons double (heavy) cream

115 g/4 oz coarsely grated sharp Cheddar cheese

Preheat the oven to 450 °F (230 °C, Gas Mark 8).

Put the oil into a large, preferably non-stick sauté pan over a medium-high heat. When hot, put in the cumin seeds. Let them sizzle for 10 seconds. Add the cauliflower florets and stir them around for 2 minutes. Add the grated tomatoes, ginger, chillies, cayenne, turmeric, ground coriander seeds and salt. Stir to mix. Stir and cook for 5–6 minutes or until the tomatoes are almost absorbed and the cauliflower almost done.

Put the contents of the pan into an oven-proof dish, about 20 cm/8 inches square, add the cream, mix, and sprinkle the cheese over the top. Put in the top third of the oven and bake for 10–12 minutes or until the cheese has melted and developed a few light-brown spots. Serve hot.

Mung Dal with Greens

Alan Ka Saag

This is an ancient (we think) family recipe made with mung beans which have been split, thus qualifying them as a *dal*, but which have not been hulled so they still have their green skins showing on one side. The addition of greens (spinach and fenugreek greens) makes this dish exceedingly nutritious, full of protein, fibre and vitamins. It's generally eaten from a small bowl (*katori*) with *phulkas* and the addition of a little butter and lime juice.

SERVES 4–6

5 tablespoons olive or other
    vegetable oil
½ teaspoon whole cumin seeds
A generous pinch of ground
    asafetida
¼ teaspoon whole fenugreek
    seeds
450 g/1 pound trimmed and
    finely chopped spinach
1 tablespoon well-crumbled
    (remove stems) dried fenu-
    greek leaves (*kasuri methi*)
250-ml/8-fl oz measure mung
    dal with skin (sold in Indian
stores as *chilkevali mung dal*),
    washed in several changes
    of water and drained
¼ teaspoon ground turmeric
1½ teaspoons salt or to taste
1 tablespoon chickpea flour
    (sometimes sold as gram
    flour or besan), mixed slowly
    with 5 tablespoons water
2 thin slices of fresh, peeled
    ginger, cut into fine slivers
2 tablespoons very fine slivers
    of peeled shallots or onion
2–4 fresh, hot green chillies

Put 2 tablespoons of the oil in a heavy-bottomed pot and set over a medium-high heat. When hot, put in the cumin seeds. Ten seconds later add the asafetida and fenugreek seeds. Stir once and quickly put in the spinach, the dried crumbled fenugreek greens, the drained split beans, turmeric and 1 litre/32 fl oz water. Stir and bring to a boil.

Watch carefully so that the contents of the pot don't boil over. Cover, leaving the lid very slightly ajar. Turn heat to low and cook very gently for 50 minutes or until the beans are tender. Add the salt and stir to mix. Stir the chickpea flour mixture and add it to the beans. Stir and cook very gently for another 10 minutes.

Put the remaining 3 tablespoons oil in a small frying pan and set over a medium-high heat. When hot, add the ginger, onion and whole green chillies. Stir-fry until the onions turn brown. Now empty the contents of the frying pan into the pot with the split beans. Stir to mix.

Stuffed Okra

We all loved this dish. It was made with young, slim pods, straight out of our garden. Even if you don't grow your own okra, look for small, tender pods. The behemoths that are sold in many grocers, with tough, fibrous skins and over-developed seeds, are good for nothing. Just pick the smallest and most delicate pods you can find.

SERVES 4–6

350 g/¾ pound whole fresh okra

1 tablespoon ground coriander seeds

1 tablespoon ground cumin seeds

1 tablespoon ground *amchoor* (ground mango powder)

¼ teaspoon cayenne pepper

½ teaspoon salt

Freshly ground black pepper

5 tablespoons olive or other vegetable oil

60 g/2 oz onion, peeled and cut into fine half-rings

Rinse the whole okra quickly and pat with paper towels until very dry. (I actually wipe each with a damp cloth, as my mother did.) You could also spread the okra out in an airy spot to dry off. Now trim the okra by cutting off the tip and either trimming off the cone-shaped top or peeling it so its shape is preserved.

In a bowl combine the coriander, cumin, *amchoor*, cayenne, salt and black pepper. Mix. Make a slit in each okra pod, ensuring you stop at least 0.5 cm/¼ inch short of the two ends and that you don't go through the whole pod. Stick a thumb into the slit to keep it open, and with the other hand take generous pinches of the seasonings and stuff them in. Stuff all the okra this way.

Use a large frying or sauté pan that can hold all the okra in a single layer (a 25-cm/10-inch pan is ideal), add the oil and set over medium-high heat. Put in the onion and stir-fry until it just begins to brown. Add all the okra in a single layer and turn the heat to medium-low. The okra should cook slowly, uncovered. Turn the okra pods gently until all sides are very lightly browned. This should take about 15 minutes. Cover the pan and turn the heat to very low for 5 minutes.

Chickpea Flour Stew with Dumplings
Karhi

A great favourite, we always ate this with plain basmati rice. *Koftas*, vegetables, salads and chutneys were always served on the side.

For this dish it helps if the yoghurt is quite sour. If I have old yoghurt sitting in the refrigerator, I tend to use that. Alternatively, I leave very fresh yoghurt in a warm place overnight and it sours sufficiently.

SERVES 6

475-ml/¾-pint measure) natural (plain) yoghurt	½ teaspoon whole cumin seeds
250-ml/8-fl oz measure or 115 g/4 oz chickpea flour (sometimes sold as gram flour or besan)	¼ teaspoon whole fennel seeds
	¼ teaspoon whole nigella seeds (sold as *kalonji*)
	15 fenugreek seeds
2 tablespoons olive or other vegetable oil	2 whole, dried, hot red chillies
	¼ teaspoon ground turmeric
	1 teaspoon salt

Put the natural yoghurt into a large bowl. Beat lightly with a fork or whisk until smooth and creamy. Slowly add 1.1 litres/2 pints water, mixing as you go.

Put the first cup of chickpea flour in another large bowl. Very slowly, add the yoghurt mixture, a little at a time, mixing as you do so. If lumps form, blend them in as you go along, before adding more liquid. If the final paste is a bit lumpy, just strain it.

Put the 2 tablespoons oil in a large pan and set over a medium heat. When hot, put in the cumin, fennel, nigella, fenugreek seeds and lastly the whole dried chillies. When the chillies darken – this takes just a few seconds – put in the turmeric and, almost immediately, the chickpea flour and yoghurt mixture. Add the salt and bring to a boil. Turn heat to low, cover partially, and simmer gently for 25 minutes. Turn off the heat.

▼▼▼

For the Dumplings

250-ml/8-fl oz measure or 115 g/4 oz chickpea flour

¼ teaspoon salt

½ teaspoon bicarbonate of soda (baking soda)

120 ml/4 fl oz natural (plain) yoghurt

Olive or other vegetable oil for deep-frying

▲▲▲

While the *karhi* is cooking, make the dumplings. Put the chickpea flour for the dumplings into a bowl. Add the salt and the bicarbonate of soda. Mix. Add the natural yoghurt and mix well with a wooden spoon. You should have a thick, droppable paste. If necessary, add another teaspoon of yoghurt. Continue to beat the paste with a wooden spoon (or a beater) for about 10 minutes or until it becomes light and airy.

Pour the oil for deep-frying into a large frying pan to a depth of about 2 cm/¾ inch. Set the pan over a medium heat. When hot, pick up a blob of paste, about 2 cm/¾ inch in diameter, on the tip of a teaspoon. Release it into the oil with the help of a second teaspoon. Make all the dumplings this way, dropping them into the oil in quick succession. Turn the dumplings around and fry them slowly until they are reddish in colour and cooked through. Remove the dumplings with a slotted spoon and spread out on a plate lined with paper towels. Let them cool slightly and then cover tightly.

Ten minutes before you sit down to eat, warm up the *karhi* over a medium heat, stirring as you go. When hot, put in all the dumplings. Cover and continue to simmer over low heat for 10 minutes.

Pumpkin

Kaddu

This appears at most of our family banquets, especially vegetarian ones. It goes particularly well with *bedvis* and *pooris*.

I find that a 1.3-kg/3-pound piece of pumpkin, with skin, yields the 900 g/2 pounds needed for this dish.

SERVES 4–6

60 ml/2 fl oz olive or other vegetable oil	2–3 dried, hot red chillies
½ teaspoon whole cumin seeds	About 900 g/2 pounds pumpkin, without skin or seeds, cut into 2.5-cm/1-inch cubes
½ teaspoon whole brown mustard seeds	
¼ teaspoon nigella seeds (*kalonji*)	¾–1 teaspoon salt
¼ teaspoon whole fennel seeds	1 ½ tablespoons light brown sugar
⅛ teaspoon whole fenugreek seeds	

Put the oil in a large, preferably non-stick pan and set over a medium-high heat. When hot, put in the cumin and mustard seeds. As soon as the mustard seeds begin to pop, a matter of seconds, add the nigella, fennel, fenugreek and red chillies. Stir once quickly and put in all the pumpkin. Stir for a minute or two. Cover, turn the heat down to low and cook for 40–45 minutes, or until just tender, stirring now and then and replacing the cover each time. Uncover and add the salt and sugar. Stir gently, mashing the pumpkin lightly to retain some texture. Serve hot.

Yoghurt with Tiny Dumplings
Boondi Ka Dahi

This yoghurt dish was served at all family weddings from a four-bowled serving apparatus with a single handle. The server flew around, doling out the yoghurt, tamarind chutney with bananas, and other relishes and pickles. We all loved the yoghurt, filled as it was with the tiniest dumplings or *boondi*, which means 'droplet'.

These days, Indian stores have taken to selling ready-made *boondi*, all fried and ready to go. They come in a bag, just like potato crisps. I have tried them out and find that they are generally stale, nothing like what you might make at home.

In India, these dumplings are made by pushing the paste through the holes of a slotted spoon directly into the hot oil. The slotted spoons there have 3-mm/⅛-inch holes. If you don't have such a spoon, use a colander or anything else with similar-sized holes.

SERVES 6–8

The Dumplings

4 heaped tablespoons chickpea flour (sometimes sold as gram flour or besan)
¼ teaspoon baking powder
¼ teaspoon salt

¼ teaspoon ground cumin seeds
Any vegetable oil for deep-frying, enough for a depth of 2.5 cm/1 inch

The Yoghurt

700 ml/24 fl oz natural
   (plain) yoghurt

1½ teaspoons salt

Freshly ground black pepper

1¼ teaspoons freshly roasted
   and ground cumin seeds

¼ teaspoon cayenne pepper

Place the chickpea flour and baking powder in a bowl. Slowly add water, about 65 ml/2¼ fl oz, and mix to a thick, smooth paste, stiff enough to stand in tiny peaks. Use a wooden spoon or your fingers to do this. Add the salt and cumin seeds and mix in. Set aside.

Put the oil for deep-frying in a 20–25-cm/8–10-inch frying pan and set over a medium heat. Have your slotted spoon or colander to hand. Fill a bowl with warm water and keep to hand as well. When the oil is hot, put a tablespoon of paste on the slotted spoon or colander and push it through with the back of a wooden spoon. Little droplets will fall into the oil. Cover the surface of the oil this way. The droplets should cook slowly, turning crisp but staying a golden yellow. They should not turn brown. This will take about 5 minutes. Adjust the heat, if necessary. As each batch gets done, remove it with a slotted spoon and transfer to the bowl of warm water. Continue until all the paste is used up. Let the dumplings soak in the water for 30 minutes.

In a bowl, mix the yoghurt well. Then add the salt, pepper, roasted cumin and cayenne, reserving a little of the cumin and cayenne for final garnishing. Cover and refrigerate the yoghurt until almost ready to serve.

Just before serving, remove a handful of dumplings from the water. Lay your other palm over them and squeeze out excess water. Do not break them. Put them in a serving dish, pour the yoghurt over them and mix gently. Sprinkle a little roasted cumin and cayenne over the top.

As a variation, if you want a slightly sweet-and-sour yoghurt, you could add 1 tablespoon sugar and 1 tablespoon sultanas (small golden raisins) that have been soaked in boiling water for an hour and then thoroughly drained.

White Radish/Mooli Relish

Churri

Served at *bedvi* and *pooris* meals in the inner city of Delhi and at all our family vegetarian feasts, this is very simple to make. All you need is white radish, also known as daikon or mooli. The more tender it is, the better. I try and get something with a diameter less than 4 cm/1½ inches. Other than that, all you need is a minimum amount of spices and lemon or lime juice.

It's best to keep the radish grated in a bowl until just before you eat. Add the seasonings towards the end as the radish tends to sweat.

SERVES 4–6

A 13-cm/5-inch segment of white radish, weighing about 140 g/5 oz	¼–½ teaspoon cayenne pepper
½ teaspoon salt	1 tablespoon lemon or lime juice
Freshly ground black pepper	

Peel the radish and grate it on the coarsest part of the grater. Just before eating, add all the other ingredients and mix well.

Light Rice Pudding

Phirni

This simple rice pudding made with ground rice grains is much loved by children and adults. In this recipe I have used rice flour, available at Indian grocers, but at home basmati rice was ground very coarsely – you could see tiny bits of rice – and then used. If you wish to do that, wash the rice first in several changes of water, drain it and spread it out to dry in the sun. Then grind it in a clean coffee-grinder.

My mother always set the pudding in shallow individual bowls, *shakoras*, made of rough terracotta. We could taste the earth in the pudding. Those days are gone now, even for most of us in Delhi!

This recipe may easily be doubled or tripled.

SERVES 4

- 5 teaspoons rice flour (also called rice powder)
- 3 tablespoons plus 475 ml/ 16 fl oz milk
- ⅛ teaspoon cardamom seeds
- 100 g/2 oz sugar, or to taste
- 1 tablespoon chopped pistachios (the shell-less, unsalted kind)

Put the rice flour in a medium bowl. Slowly add the 3 tablespoons milk and mix to a smooth paste.

Set the remaining 475 ml/16 fl oz milk to boil in a heavy, small-ish pan, over a medium-low heat. Crush the cardamom seeds in a mortar and add them, as well as the sugar, to the milk. As soon as the milk begins to boil and rise, remove it from the heat. Stir the rice paste in the bowl once again. Slowly pour the hot milk into the bowl with the rice paste, mixing with a whisk as you do so. Now pour the contents of the bowl back into the pan, place over a low heat and bring to a simmer. Stir frequently with a whisk and simmer very gently for about 15 minutes. Pour into 4 shallow, individual bowls and allow to cool and set slightly. Sprinkle the pistachios over the top and refrigerate. Serve cold.

Fresh Limeade

Neebu Ka Sharbat

Indian limes are juicy and small. Use whatever limes you can find.

MAKES 1 TALL GLASS

5 tablespoons freshly squeezed
lime juice

4 tablespoons very fine sugar

Water, plain or fizzy

Ice cubes

Mix the lime juice and sugar in a small bowl. Let the sugar dissolve completely. Pour into a tall glass. Pour in 175 ml/6 fl oz water, either plain or fizzy, and add a few ice cubes. Stir.

AUTHOR'S
ACKNOWLEDGEMENTS

❋ ❋ ❋

I would like to thank the following for all their help
in putting this book together:

Anupjija, Krishna, Inder Bhabi and Ajay, Santoshjiji, Suresh,
Madhu, Bimla, Lovy, Shashi, Om, Brijdada, Bhaiyyadada, Maya
and Siddhartha, Lalit, Kamal, Ruth Jhabwala, Anita Desai,
Amitav Ghosh, and Viru and Juji Dayal.

I would also like to offer thanks to the *New Yorker*,
Gourmet magazine, the *Financial Times* and *Ms. Magazine*, from
which some lines, thoughts and words have been taken.

PUBLISHER'S ACKNOWLEDGEMENTS

❀ ❀ ❀

The Publishers would like to thank Nandan Jha and
Rahul Srivastava for their help in Delhi, and Lalit and Maya Jaggi
for their help in London.

ABOUT THE AUTHOR

❀ ❀ ❀

Now regarded by many as the world authority on Indian food,
Madhur Jaffrey was born in Delhi and began her career as an
actress. She wrote her first book in 1974 and in 1982 her series
for BBC television, *Madhur Jaffrey's Indian Cookery*, made her into a
household name. She has written over 15 bestselling
cookery books, including *Madhur Jaffrey's World Vegetarian*,
Madhur Jaffrey's Step-by-Step Cookery, *Madhur Jaffrey's Quick and Easy
Indian Cookery*, and *Madhur Jaffrey's Ultimate Curry Bible*,
voted Cookery Book of the Year 2004 by the Guild of Food
Writers and also published by Ebury Press.

ALSO BY MADHUR JAFFREY

❀ ❀ ❀

Madhur Jaffrey's Ultimate Curry Bible
The definitive curry book by the world authority on Indian food

Madhur Jaffrey's Quick and Easy Indian Cookery
Over 75 delicious recipes that can be cooked in 30 minutes or less,
demonstrating the versatility of authentic Indian cuisine

Madhur Jaffrey's Step-by-Step Cookery
Over 150 dishes from India and the Far East, including
Thailand, Vietnam and Malaysia

Madhur Jaffrey's World Vegetarian
An unrivalled sourcebook of over 600 recipes and ingredients
from all over the globe

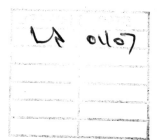